IGNITE

ANDRE DE GRASSE

IGNITE

UNLOCK THE HIDDEN POTENTIAL WITHIN

WITH DAN ROBSON

HarperCollinsPublishersLtd

Published by HarperCollins Publishers Ltd

First edition

HarperCollins books may be purchased for educational, business,
or sales promotional use through our Special Markets Department.

HarperCollins Publishers Ltd
Bay Adelaide Centre, East Tower
22 Adelaide Street West, 41st Floor
Toronto, Ontario, Canada
M5H 4E3

www.harpercollins.ca

Library and Archives Canada Cataloguing in Publication

Title: Ignite : unlock the hidden potential within /
Andre De Grasse ; with Dan Robson.
Names: De Grasse, Andre, 1994- author. | Robson, Dan, 1983- author.
Identifiers: Canadiana (print) 20230460925 | Canadiana (ebook) 2023046100X |
ISBN 9781443469074 (hardcover) | ISBN 9781443469081 (ebook)
Subjects: LCSH: De Grasse, Andre, 1994- | LCSH: Sprinters—Canada—Biography.
LCSH: Self-actualization (Psychology) | LCSH: Determination (Personality trait)
LCGFT: Autobiographies.
Classification: LCC GV1061.15.D4 A3 2023 | DDC 796.42/2092—dc23

Printed and bound in the United States of America
23 24 25 26 27 LBC 5 4 3 2 1

To everyone who has the courage to follow their dreams

CONTENTS

IGNITE

1

A BLUR IN SLOW MOTION

There is a quiet that fills the air right before the gun goes off. It's the moment when everything is on the line—as people often say—and all the work you've put in up to that single crack of a starter's pistol is finally tested.

Everything, all at once.

All the hours spent on the track, perfecting the tiniest variations in your stride that might give you an edge. All those hours in the gym, working to build just a little more explosiveness out of the blocks—a push that just might nudge you ahead. All of the years following a strict regimen, making sure your body is as primed and ready for this moment as possible.

It's more than all of that though. It's not just the physical work. Or the pain that sets in—the pain you must push through, because you know your competitors will too. It's not just the exhaustion that always follows. Or the disappointments when the extra speed you're searching for just doesn't come.

It's also the weight of expectation. It's knowing you can be the fastest person to reach the line ahead, and knowing so many people watching believe you can too. It's the fear of letting yourself and those people down. It's knowing there is only one outcome that won't also carry some level of disappointment.

It's remembering the days when it seemed as though moments like this would never return. The feeling that your body had betrayed you. When injuries seemed too insurmountable for you to ever get back the strength you had before. It's knowing how that doubt crept in, the way doubt always tries to—even in the most seemingly confident people—and having to fight back with all the positivity you can find within you and beyond you. It's remembering all the people who've stood behind you on that line, believing in you, supporting you, challenging you, embracing you—loving you. It's knowing that without the blessing of those people in your life, you would have never been able to stand here at all.

Everything carries a lot.

But right now everything is on the line, and the world around me goes quiet. This is where and when I really come to life.

Somewhere in those fractions of a second, something ignites inside of me, fuelled by everything that came before. *Crack*—and I'm a rocket ripping towards the finish line as fast as a human body is capable.

The first few seconds often predict the outcome. You know the game plan. It was forged through many victories and defeats. It was the focus of thousands of sessions on the track, in the gym, of studying the strengths and weaknesses of the world's fastest men beside me. You know that *your* strength is your top-end speed, and that if you can just get a good start and stick with the pack rushing beside you, the race is yours.

But sometimes the game plan doesn't go as intended. Everyone else is working from a game plan of their own. The people beside you are being propelled by the force of everything behind them too—all the work, all the hope, all the same desires to be the best— and they are doing everything in this brief flash of time to beat you and all the others.

All you can hear is the thunder of 14 feet, besides your own, and a glimpse of bodies trying to push past the corners of your eyes. You can feel your heart pounding. You can feel the air filling and escaping your lungs. You can feel the pierce of lactic acid pain in your legs.

You can't tell who pulls ahead and who lags. But you can tell *when* someone does. And you can feel the panic when it seems like your plan isn't working.

The conversation begins. You tell yourself you've got to stay calm.

Relax, pump your arms . . . Relax, pump your arms . . .
Hit the ground . . . Hit the ground . . .
Stand up tall . . . Don't sit . . . Keep the hips up . . .
Stay relaxed . . . Always stay relaxed . . .

That's when everything slows down in your mind. But panic has rarely been strong enough to defeat me. If anything, it drives me. And now you're hunting, determined to catch that body and blow past it.

At the same time, you need to maintain your rhythm. It's so important in sprinting. It's all about the feel of your body operating like a finely tuned machine. The speed might increase, but without the symmetry of that stride—that rhythm—the entire system falls apart. In the final stretch of any sprint everyone slows down, but some slow down less. A race is won in the ability to hold your speed longer than everyone else.

The last 20 metres are about finishing the hunt. Keeping pace, maintaining form, but bursting with a final push of power.

This is going to be close . . .

A few more strides.

Lean, lean . . . Lean!

////////

I'm on a mission to be the fastest sprinter I can be, to execute to my full potential. I know my best race is yet to come. But this book isn't about my pursuit of medals or records on the track; it's about what I've learned along the way.

When I look back, sometimes life feels like a blur too. It's hard to identify all those steps that have led me onto the podium at multiple Olympic Games and World Athletics Championships, or the missteps that resulted in a near career-ending hamstring injury. But ultimately, these steps, good and bad, led me to become a champion. They've also built my life beyond the track, starting a family of my own and working to be the best kind of father and man I can be.

In writing this book, I've attempted to slow it all down and try to distill the lessons I've learned throughout my pursuit of excellence on and off the track.

I've been fortunate to learn from so many great people in my life. From my mother to my girlfriend and closest friends, to my management team, trainers, doctors, therapists, teammates, and mentors, and to the dedicated coaches who have supported and guided me along the way. If there is one thing I've learned more than anything, it's that I've been blessed in this life by the people around me.

In many ways, what I've experienced as a high-performance athlete has been applicable to how I live my life. I've been through many disappointments in my career so far. I've made mistakes and faced challenges that seemed insurmountable at times. I've battled with anxieties and found myself in deep valleys consumed with doubt. But I've also found success, working through that adversity to reach the goals I set out to achieve. I've learned how to look at what seems impossible and truly believe I can accomplish it. And I've managed to find balance and feel at peace as I take on those challenges.

In other words, I've found a rhythm of life that works for me. I've learned to keep disappointment and success in perspective, knowing that more of each will come regardless of what I do.

As I've slowed everything down to work through this book, I've come to understand more about myself. I've come to see where I can be better, but also where I can find more satisfaction and contentment.

I've shared the lessons I've learned along the way here. These lessons are not chronological. This book is not a memoir. Instead, I've gathered individual stories from all aspects and periods of my life so I can share a road map to reveal some of the ways I've managed to achieve success.

I hope you might find these reflections on life and learning useful in your own pursuit of greatness—as a high-performance athlete, in your career, or just in each day of a life well lived. I also hope the lessons I've learned while striving to achieve my goals will be helpful to you as you reach for yours.

I'm only partway through my journey. I'm still learning how to be the best man, the best father, and the best athlete I can be. I still have more to achieve on the track—and much more to achieve in this life. In the end, I hope my legacy is measured by what I achieve in both.

As I continue that pursuit, thank you for taking time out of life's busy pace to slow it all down with me.

2

THE ACCIDENTAL SPRINTER

What the hell am I going to do with my life?

That was the question that filled my every day as I rode the bus around the city dropping off resumés during my senior year of high school at Milliken Mills in Markham, Ontario. I was facing that scary part of a young person's life where suddenly the future seems very close and very uncertain.

It was the start of the most important lessons I've learned. Without that question, it's likely you wouldn't be reading about my life at all.

When I was young, I dreamed of playing in the NBA. I grew up watching the Toronto Raptors, idolizing guys like Vince Carter and Tracy McGrady. I definitely drew inspiration from them. My mom got an artist to paint the Raptors logo on my wall. So I was a big fan. But more than that, I had a hoop dream. I had been certain I was going to play in the NBA one day. Of course, I wasn't the only one. All of my friends loved sports. That was where I found my closest connections—playing soccer, baseball, hockey, and basketball outside for hours. And we all dreamed of growing up to be like the stars we admired. Some of us wanted to be in the NHL or play MLB. But Andre De Grasse? He was going to be an NBA star.

As a teenager, I played for two different Amateur Athletic Union (AAU) travel teams from Toronto, the top tier of competitive ball. A newspaper photo emerged early in my career of me driving against future NBAer Andrew Wiggins in a game between our high schools. But the picture told only part of the story: Wiggins fouled me on the bucket. Unfortunately that was as close to a poster moment as I'd get in the sport I loved most as a kid.

I was an undersized guard, but I was fast. I was a vocal player on the court, always trying to lead my team. I've always had a competitive edge. I was the kind of guy who refused to let up, even in pickup games. If I lost, we were playing until I won. And I took it as seriously as I knew how, at the time, as a teenager. I knew I was athletic and that I had talent. There was nothing I was more passionate about than playing ball.

I wanted to earn a scholarship to an NCAA (National Collegiate Athletic Association) school, because that was where all the best Canadian players were going. I wanted a chance to play in front of thousands of wild fans, like we saw on TV every year watching March Madness. And after that, I wanted to play in the NBA—just like those players on my wall.

But the truth is, I wasn't prepared to put in the effort it would take to reach that level. At the time, I didn't have the kind of work ethic it requires to make it to the next level of any sport. Desire alone is never enough, but I didn't understand that then. What I knew was that everyone always told me I was good at basketball. And in that world, I was. But I never practised hard. I thought my talent alone would be enough to carry me along.

As I went through high school, I started to notice the incredible improvement that some other players were making. They were talented too, but suddenly they were reaching the next level. By the time I realized the reason they were getting so much better was because they were putting in the work—practising hard on the court, training in the gym, dedicating their lives to basketball—it was too late. These were guys I had been better than, but now they had a step on me. They were smarter and stronger on the court. They had the edge.

That didn't click for me until my senior year, and by that time there was no going back. It was already clear I wasn't on the radar of NCAA schools the way I'd felt I deserved to be. That was when I first started to understand how much time I'd lost goofing off when I should have been working towards my goals. While part of me wishes I'd learned that lesson sooner, I also know that sometimes it's just not meant to be.

In high school, class never captured my attention. I had a difficult time focusing. My mind always raced to different places during lectures. I found myself daydreaming about playing basketball, or being distracted by friends. It wasn't that school was particularly challenging. I just didn't apply myself. I was too immature at the time—consumed by the naivety of youth—to see the need for school. The only area I was focused on was basketball. I put all my focus into that dream, at the expense of working hard in school.

I got by on my athleticism but lacked the work ethic of other players in the AAU circuit. I watched these guys improve, adding to their strengths and fixing their weaknesses. They'd learned the key to improvement, which is a lesson it took me too long to understand.

In my final semester, I enrolled in a co-op placement, which allowed me to collect credits that I needed to graduate, because I wasn't interested in spending any more time in the classroom. As part of the program, we needed to hand out resumés and land a volunteer job to fulfill the requirements.

By that time, when I was riding the city bus with a stack of resumés, I knew I wasn't going to land the NCAA scholarship I'd hoped for. Despite it being my passion, in my heart I knew that basketball was coming to an end. The basketball season was cancelled in my Grade 12 year at Milliken Mills, so I was playing only the AAU and OBA (Ontario Basketball Association) circuit at the time. The world of competitive sports is full of politics and tough to navigate. I didn't have anyone to help me navigate it, to help me land a scholarship or get to the next level.

My mother encouraged me to keep playing, even to stick around high school for a fifth year to try to get my grades up and play another season of ball. She could see me wandering off the right track and wanted to keep me from making big mistakes while I was young. To be blunt, I spent a lot of time hanging out with friends, chasing girls, and smoking weed. It was fun, but it was misguided. It was a waste.

My mother sat me down and asked whether I wanted to keep focusing on my basketball dream or whether it was better to give up the sport and focus my energy on pursuing a practical career. She knew that basketball wasn't going to pay my bills. Maybe, she said, I could attend college or university in Canada and try to make a varsity team, while studying in a program I liked. I dismissed that idea.

My mom didn't really know about the NCAA, I thought. *That's where you have to make it happen.* I could only see one route worth taking in basketball—the NCAA—and it was apparent that opportunity had passed me by. Even though I was still playing on the side, I knew there likely wasn't a future in the sport for me. I'd missed my chance to make the most of the talent and opportunity I'd been given.

That realization was probably one of the most critical moments in my life. I didn't have the grades to go to university. And even if I did, I had no idea what I'd want to study. I thought about maybe becoming a mechanic, because I loved cars. I also thought it would be cool to be a gym teacher. And I'd started to have some interest in social work.

Whichever direction I went, this was a decision I was going to need to make on my own. What did I plan to do with the rest of my life?

I remember the moment clearly. It was so random. I was riding the bus to hand out resumés after another long day of my co-op placement when my good friend Mikhile got on.

"What's up, man? How've you been?" I asked.

"Yeah, I'm good, man. I'm good," he said. "Where are you headed?"

I told him about job hunting and about how I wasn't sure what I was going to do when school was over. Mikhile was on his way to track practice at York University, where he'd joined a running club. He took track seriously. He was getting ready for an upcoming meet. I'd teased Mikhile, telling him he wasn't that fast and that I could beat him. Mikhile challenged me to prove it.

Why not?

I told him I would. Our buddy Zach was also planning to run. He wanted to add track to his sporting resumé so he could win the Athlete of the Year award at his high school. Mikhile was trying to connect with a girl who ran track. The track meets were all-day affairs away from school. When you weren't competing, you sat in the stands watching others race and hanging out with friends.

I signed up for the team at Milliken Mills. It wasn't hard to qualify for a high school track team in Canada at the time. It wasn't a popular sport like basketball. As long as you were decently athletic, you could compete.

The York Region District championships, our school district north of Toronto, were held at the track complex at York University. That morning, I told my mom I was heading to a track meet.

"Track?" she said. "Shouldn't you be in school?"

I told her, no, I was going to be running with the track team that day. Mom smiled and joked that I just wanted to get away from school for a day. And to be fair, she was right. I showed up expecting a chill day with my friends. I was signed up for the 100-metre race but didn't expect much to come of it. There were about 100 other runners that day. We were all grouped in heats that ran one after the other.

My friends knew I was fast because they'd seen me on a soccer pitch and basketball court. A few times we'd had to sprint in real life, after goofing around like teenage boys often do and needing to get away fast. But I hadn't run a 100-metre race since middle school. I showed up in basketball shorts and borrowed a pair of spikes. I wore a black T-shirt underneath my Milliken Mills singlet. Before the race, I was given the number 635, which I pinned to my singlet.

When I was called out for my heat, I watched the other runners line up on the starting blocks. I had never heard of starting blocks before, let alone used them. When the starter told everyone to "get set," I just crouched sideways like I was about to dash from first base to second base, while everyone else set themselves up properly. I don't know what the other guys in the race thought of me, but I imagine they didn't think I was going to be much competition. When the starter's pistol went off, I started to run as fast as I could. I didn't know anything about sprinting, but I knew a lot about competing. I just wanted to run faster than every guy beside me.

The laces of my borrowed shoes came undone before I reached the finish line. If I had stepped on them by mistake, I could have fallen flat on my face in front of everybody. And that would have been it for my track career—my day would have ended with severely wounded pride. Thankfully, that didn't happen. I crossed the line and realized I'd won my heat!

I was as shocked as everyone else. I was thrilled. But aside from a win for my self-esteem, I couldn't have dreamed that anything else would come from it. But I had earned a spot in the final.

The favourite to win was a guy named Bolade Ajomale, who was already known as one of the top sprinters in the country (and would later go on to win bronze with me in the 4 x 100-metre relay at the Rio Olympics).

Tony Sharpe arrived at York University just a few minutes before the race. Tony competed at the Los Angeles Olympics in 1984, winning a bronze medal in the 4 x 100-metre relay. He also set a Canadian record in the 200 metres. In retirement, he'd become one of the most renowned sprinting coaches in Canada. He ran an academy that trained young talent he found, turning them into some of the best sprinters in the country.

Tony was at the event to watch one of his athletes, Josh Cunningham, who was also from Markham and was a top 400-metre runner who went on to become a senior national champion in the event. Tony arrived just in time to catch the senior boys' 100-metre final, which happened before the 400-metre final. Had he been a few minutes later, he would have missed it completely.

But that day, as I lined up at the starting blocks at the York Region District championships, crouching awkwardly while the others got set, Tony stood on the sidelines. He always had an interest in finding undiscovered talent. A big part of his academy was recruiting high school kids who didn't realize they could have a future in track.

Tony first noticed me as I stood next to the other runners, looking sideways at the starter while the rest all leaned forward and looked ahead. The gun went off and I started to run. I didn't win the race, so I didn't think much of it, other than that it was cool that I showed up for my first track meet and made it to the finals. My second-place finish qualified me to advance to the regional finals, which meant my very young track career would continue.

But my time of 10.97 was enough to catch Tony's attention. It was clear from my start and from my unconventional form that I had received no prior coaching. Running sub-11 seconds without any training met the threshold for someone who was naturally very fast. If I had been a Grade 9 student, I would have been the perfect candidate for Tony to bring to his academy and train for several years with the aim of becoming a provincial or national champion. But I was already in Grade 12. What potential really existed for me?

However, Tony started asking around about me. Josh Cunningham told him my name was Tip. That's what all my friends called me back then, and what a lot of them still do. He learned I had absolutely no training as a sprinter before that day. He asked Josh, whom I'd played ball with, to introduce us. Later that afternoon, Josh brought Tony across the field to the tents where my school team was stationed.

"This is my track coach, Tony," Josh said.

Tony introduced himself.

"Hey, guess what, dude. You got something special going on here," he said.

I didn't know what to say. I knew I'd surprised some people with my race and I felt great about it. But at that point it still hadn't crossed my mind that this was anything more than a fun way to end my high school days.

"I'd like to help you going forward," he said. "Because there is no way you're going to beat my six sprinters in the next round."

I didn't know what to think. Was he kidding me? Did this man actually want to train me? Did he really think I had a shot to do something as a sprinter? And what does that even look like? I knew nothing about the sport.

Tony handed me his card. He told me he was running a session the next Saturday morning at a high school nearby. He wanted to teach me how to properly sprint from the starting blocks. There was no way I was going to beat his guys with a standing start. I told

Tony I appreciated his interest, not entirely sure what to make of it. I tucked the card in the pocket of my backpack and went home.

Tony wasn't sure whether he'd ever hear from me again. He was always recruiting and knew a lot of these conversations didn't end up going anywhere. Finding talent is one thing, but finding talent that wanted to be taught and to learn was another thing altogether. If this had happened a couple of years earlier, I might not have thought much of the opportunity. There's a good chance I still would have been too focused on basketball to consider taking on the kind of commitment it would take to practise track to have a future in it. And at the time, I didn't even know what a possible future in track looked like.

But I'd just experienced the exhilaration of sprinting. I was surprised by the adrenalin rush of the competition. I was surprised by how happy I was about doing so well, unexpectedly. I'd been in such a discouraged state of mind. Anxious about my future for the first time, I suddenly had someone telling me I had a chance to do something special, even if it was just a small chance. I wasn't going to let this one go.

When I went home that night, I told my mom about the race. She was happy I'd done so well and to see me be so enthusiastic about it. My mother had always come to the small track meets I was in while in elementary school (back when every student ran in track meets). She was a sprinter in the 100 and 200 metres in high school in Trinidad, where she grew up. She wanted me to keep running track when I got to high school, but I showed little interest—until now.

I told her about Tony Sharpe, that he was an Olympian who thought I had actual potential. Mom had never heard of him before (and neither had I), so she was a little bit skeptical. My mother has always been protective of me, which probably has to do with me being an only child. Throughout my career she's been a shrewd observer and a voice of wisdom, someone who always has my best interests at heart and is wary of anyone who doesn't seem to.

I asked my mom to give Tony a call for me. She took his card and said she would. I don't think she realized how serious I was. She was wary about encouraging me to get too caught up in the excitement, because I was about to finish high school. Mom thought I should be thinking about college and worried that my new interest in sprinting was going to be a distraction. I was a young man now, she thought. It was time for me to think about getting a job and starting a career. It was time for me to step into adulthood. Mom put the card in her purse, thinking I'd likely forget all about it the next day. But I was persistent. The next morning, I called her while she was at work and asked if she'd spoken with Tony yet.

"Andre, I'm working," she said. "I can't call him now."

She promised to call him on her lunch break.

Tony told my mother that he wished he'd met me a year earlier. He told her I had the natural talent to be a top sprinter in the province, even though all the top-tier competition had already been training for years. He asked her to bring me to Bill Crothers Secondary School that Saturday morning, when he was running a practice for his club. It was the school my mother had tried to get me into when she had me transfer out of the local Catholic school because I was getting too distracted. The school specialized in high-performance athletics, but I wasn't accepted into the program and ended up at Milliken Mills instead.

That Saturday morning, my mom and I met Tony at the track. She took a seat in the stands and watched, just as she always had whenever I had a basketball practice.

Tony worked with me for about 40 minutes, going over the very basic mechanics of running. He showed me how to set up on the blocks and how to take off on the gun. I absorbed everything Tony said. I think it was because I knew I had no business being there. I didn't have an ego in track because I hadn't had the time to develop one. All I knew was that an Olympic medallist was offering to make me better—and I couldn't afford to mess this opportunity up.

A couple weeks later, I ran in a regional qualifier known as "the centrals" and landed a spot in the Ontario Federation of School Athletic Associations (OFSAA) provincial championships. I asked my mother to make the trip to Brockville, four hours east, to watch me compete.

Mom made the trip with her niece. They drove out to Brockville in the morning, expecting I wouldn't make it to the final and they could be home in time for dinner. But I made it through the first round, and they had to stick around. Everyone there seemed to know my story. They were watching to see if I was for real. Later that day, I won the second round and earned a spot in the final, much to everyone's surprise, including my own. There were a lot more people at the provincial championships than there had been at the district and regional qualifiers. As far as Ontario athletics go, the OFSAA championships was our Olympics, known to be one of the most competitive high school championship meets in the world. Every other guy on the line with me in the final was en route to run track for an NCAA school the next year. I had started running less than a month earlier and was wavering about whether I'd try to land a job the following year or give college a try.

I placed sixth.

I was calm about the result. I wasn't upset, but I wasn't happy. Most importantly, I wasn't done. In just a few short weeks, I stepped into a new challenge and learned something about myself I hadn't realized before. It wasn't just that I was fast. That was only part of it. It was that I'd taken on a challenge and worked at it with everything I had. In that short span, I'd worked constantly with Tony as he patiently showed me how to start off the blocks, over and over, and mapped out the intricacies of my stride. I still had terrible form and a lot to learn, but even the small improvements were enough to make me feel like the progress made the hard work worth it.

I decided I was willing to take a chance on me. I was going to jump out into the unknown and make the most of whatever came from it.

After the provincials, I continued to work with Tony several times a week. But soon school was over, and I was officially out in the real world. Without another year of high school, I didn't have an avenue for showing improvement. Still, I returned to Tony, finding hope in his belief in me and my ability. He told me an international track meet was taking place at the University of Toronto's Varsity Stadium less than two weeks after the provincial championships. The meet organizers decided to include a special 100-metre race featuring some of the top high school sprinters. Using his connections in the track and field community, Tony managed to get me into that race. I didn't find this out until many years later, but the guy he called was Brian Levine, the meet promoter, who would later become a key part of my management team, looking after most of my endorsements, public relations, and charitable work.

All three provincial OFSAA medallists were in the race. The meet director gave me lane eight—the last lane on the far edge of the track, which no runner wants to be in—but they squeezed me in at the last minute so there wasn't much to complain about. I already knew I was an outsider there. This time, instead of worrying about my competition I lined up in the blocks, running through everything Tony had taught me.

I can't remember much about the actual race, but I remember what happened next very well. As I crossed the finish line, I realized there was no one in front of me. I'd beaten all three provincial medallists from just a few weeks earlier. It was an insane upset. Nobody at Varsity Stadium that day expected that outcome. When I was called up to the podium a short time later, I didn't even know where to stand. I just stood beside the silver and bronze medal winners, while they tried to nudge me to the top riser.

"No, no, no," one said. "You won. You go in the middle."

That was the day I realized I could make something of myself in this sport. But as far as the sport went, I was almost completely out of time to make that happen. I'd bet on myself and taken a chance at something new, but it seemed too late for anything meaningful to come of it. I was way behind in my development, compared with most of my competitors who had already been training for years. Most sprinters my age had already been recruited for university programs in the United States and Canada.

Still, I felt inspired to keep going. I loved the thrill of the competition and the rush of winning. Maybe there was still an outside chance to make something happen. Tony encouraged me to keep training. For the next couple of weeks, Mom drove me out to each practice and training session with him. He continued to build on what he'd taught me. We worked constantly, repeating each action on the blocks over and over.

"React to the whistle!" he'd shout as I lined up on the block to refine my starts.

"Again . . . Again . . . Again."

I kept working, not knowing what the outcome would be—or if there would be any real outcome at all.

It was an act of blind faith. The kind of faith in yourself that you need in order to take hold of the opportunities that come your way.

Soon I'd be given another opportunity to take a leap of faith. Without my taking that step into the unknown, it's unlikely you'd know my story at all.

When you are given a chance to pursue something exciting, jump at it. Even if it might seem as though there is a very small likelihood that you will succeed. Never let your doubt or apathy stop you from unlocking your potential.

This was one of the first lessons I learned in my sprint towards greatness. I think about how close I came to never having run in that first high school race at all. I think about how easy it would have been to have stuffed Tony's card in my pocket and never given it a second thought. What a waste that would have been. After I made the decision to train that year and shocked myself by reaching the OFSAA final, I could have just left it at that. As I said, I was way behind as a sprinter. At the time, it seemed like there was almost too much ground to make up.

But I took a chance and bet on myself anyway. I might be known as "the accidental sprinter" because of my unlikely journey, but there is nothing accidental about what I've achieved in track. I made the decision to believe I was able to achieve something that seemed nearly impossible.

Even though the odds were against me, if I hadn't tried I would have walked away from track with nothing more than a fun story about my final year in high school. Greatness can only be achieved if you take advantage of opportunities when they come, regardless of how unexpected or unlikely they might seem.

What about you?

Are there goals you've dreamed of achieving but have never taken a step towards accomplishing? What is getting in your way?

Is it fear?

Is it doubt?

Is it apathy?

Don't let any of those self-restricting emotions block you from pursuing your destiny. You will never know your full potential if you don't make the choice to believe you can achieve great things. You will never show the world just how much you are capable of if you don't take advantage of opportunities when they arise. And you will never succeed unless you decide to truly believe you can.

3

SPEAK IT INTO EXISTENCE

Coffeyville Community College doesn't come up very often when people ask me about my story, but in many ways, that was where my journey as an athlete really took shape.

Several years ago, I sat in my room in the dormitory apartment I shared with three other guys, in what seemed like the middle of nowhere.

Coffeyville has a population of less than nine thousand people, which of course is quite a contrast to the nearly six million people who live in the Greater Toronto Area, where I grew up. The town is an industry and manufacturing hub in the southeastern part of Kansas, which is a state I wouldn't have been able to point out on a map before I moved there as a 17-year-old, leaving home for the first time.

The college itself is just a little bit larger than the high school I went to. But Coffeyville is known for its athletics. The school had produced more than 48 NFL players, including running back Mike

Rozier, who went on to win the Heisman Trophy and became a two-time Pro Bowl running back. Buster Douglas, the boxer who became heavyweight champion after knocking out Mike Tyson in 1990, played basketball for Coffeyville.

I was away from home for the very first time, enrolled in a community college in a small town in Kansas. At the time I had no idea what lay ahead for me as an athlete or as a student. Less than a year earlier, I'd never even thought about running track.

It was clear that I had natural talent, but I was still relatively new to the sport and needed a lot of refinement if I was going to improve in any meaningful way. I'd finished high school a couple of months earlier, in June 2012, and had just started to make a name for myself in Canadian track. I didn't have anywhere else to go if I wanted to continue competing at a high level.

That August, I'd received a Facebook message from a man named Robert Wood, asking if I'd be interested in attending the junior college in Kansas, where he was the director of student life and assistant coach for the school's track and field team. It was such a random message that I wasn't quite sure what to make of it. I showed my mother, who took his email and reached out to him within the hour. My mom, Beverley, always wanted me to pursue an education. But with average high school grades and my late arrival as a high school track athlete, it didn't seem likely that I could go the collegiate route in the States. The likeliest option was that I'd use my new-found talent to attend college in Ontario and possibly transfer over to a university. But Coach Wood was looking for a new recruit after other athletes had backed out a few weeks before school started. He already had three other sprinters from the Toronto area entering his program, so he searched online to see if there was any overlooked talent. My name popped up.

After Coach Wood and my mother spoke, she connected him with Tony Sharpe, the coach who discovered me. Tony assured us that the unexpected opportunity at Coffeyville was the best chance I had to make something out of being a sprinter.

I wasn't familiar with the concept of junior college at the time. For athletes, it's considered a stepping stone to an NCAA scholarship. This system in the States gives students a second chance at post-secondary education, after missing out on going directly to college for a variety of reasons. It could be an academic deficiency or because a student has run into some social trouble. In many cases, it is simply a matter of finances. Junior college is a much cheaper route than university. For students coming from the state, tuition is less than $2,000 for a year, whereas the University of Kansas can cost up to $30,000. Students typically attend junior college for two years before being able to move on to a larger college program. Coffeyville, specifically, had earned a reputation as a place where athletes hoping to reach the next level could improve their academics, while still excelling in sports, in order to land the scholarship they'd previously missed out on. If you've ever watched *Last Chance U* on Netflix, it's a lot like that.

I spoke with my mother about it. She wasn't sure she wanted me to leave home—something I'd never done before. We were both uncertain about me heading to a small farming community in the middle of nowhere.

But this opportunity must have come our way for a reason. For me, it seemed like a second chance to chase my crumbled basketball dream. My unexpected emergence in track, at the very last possible minute before I finished high school, offered me an opportunity to earn an athletic scholarship in the NCAA.

The conversations between Coach Wood, Tony, and my mother centred primarily around academics. Tony vouched for what Coach Wood had read about my ability on the track. I had raw talent that just needed to be refined. But at Coffeyville, there is a firm focus on academics, and if I wasn't going to be committed in the classroom, there was no point in heading to Kansas. Coach Wood stressed that the primary goal for any student accepted to Coffeyville was to graduate. Many of the students had a history of struggling academically, and the school was committed to helping each of them realize their value and worth in the classroom. That meant there were strict standards when it came to grades—and if you didn't make the grades, you weren't eligible to play. Coffeyville has said goodbye to many students over the years because of that standard. Coach Wood wanted to be sure I wasn't one of them.

But with this unexpected second chance, there was no way I was going to let that happen. The hope was I'd do well enough in class and on the track at Coffeyville that I might be able to earn a full scholarship to run track for a top NCAA school after two years.

It wasn't an NCAA scholarship, but it was a start and a path to getting there. All I needed to do was move to the middle of nowhere in a new country, keep my grades, and run fast enough that I was impossible to ignore.

This was the chance I'd been waiting for just a few months earlier when I pondered what I planned to do with the rest of my life. Even though it would mean leaving home, it was Mom who gave me the courage to step into a new unknown.

"Go do it. Make it happen. Your education might get paid for," she told me. "And beyond that—who knows?"

Within days, we all agreed I'd head to Coffeyville, Kansas—a place I'd never dreamed of being, with an opportunity I'd never imagined possible.

///////

Growing up in a massive region like Toronto and its surrounding suburbs, I definitely wasn't prepared for the quiet isolation of Coffeyville. Coach Wood picked me up at the airport in Tulsa, Oklahoma, when I first arrived. It's an hour-and-a-half drive across state lines to Coffeyville, but Tulsa is the closest airport around. We passed wide-open fields—more land than I'd ever seen before. Enormous pumps, pulling oil from the earth, popped up every now and then on the horizon across those expansive fields.

When we rolled in that Saturday night the town was still. Almost eerily quiet. It was tinier than anyplace I'd been before. Needless to say, it was just the beginning of a serious culture shock. Even after I'd arrived and was living there for a while, I still wasn't quite sure where the hell Coffeyville was.

I lived in a quad with the few other Canadians on the track team. That also helped me deal with the culture shock I was experiencing. None of us knew each other before we arrived, because we were all from different parts of Toronto. But very quickly, it seemed like we'd grown up together—given how far away from home we were, both geographically and culturally.

We were all in similar places in our lives. Every person I met at Coffeyville was trying to turn their life around, get their grades up—and trying to go to the NCAA to make their dreams come true, whether that was making it to MLB, the NBA, or the NFL. There was nothing to do in Coffeyville other than trying to hang out with girls and partying. Some people would get distracted, spending too much time on their social life. But as much as I appreciated the connection I'd made with my roommates, I didn't have time to focus on hanging out or goofing around.

There was work to do. Coffeyville gave me a chance and I wasn't going to blow it. This was a big opportunity. It was also a huge step in my life. Not only was I on my own in a brand new place, but the outcome was unknown. There were no guarantees I'd be able to make something of myself on the track, despite Tony's belief in me. The scholarship covered tuition, so at the very least I was gaining an education. But we still had to pay for boarding, food, and other living expenses like that. That meant my mother was footing the bill from back home, sending her only child away to make something of his life. It was a huge adjustment: living with roommates, learning how to make my own meals, keeping my grades up to keep my scholarship.

But in that four-room dorm I shared with three other Canadian kids chasing track dreams through Kansas, I sat down and remembered a mantra a friend of mine had told me several years before: "speak it into existence."

The truth is, for all my swagger on the basketball court and with my friends, I wasn't a very confident young man before I left for Coffeyville. I wasn't quite certain what to believe about myself. Beyond basketball, I didn't have a sense of what my talents were— or what my unique strengths could achieve. I was directionless.

I now know it is commonplace for any person in their late teens and early twenties to find themselves like this. I wasn't alone in the insecurities I felt, even though insecurities always feel isolating.

When I first had a coach tell me they thought I might be able to go pro in track as I neared the end of high school, it opened my eyes to a possibility I hadn't considered before. When people tell you that you actually have a shot, it changes your perspective and provides you with a new kind of confidence.

When I'd first heard the phrase "speak it into existence," I kind of tucked it away as a motivational saying that just meant if I really wanted to do something, I could achieve it. But with a bit of age and experience—and yes, disappointment—I'd started to think about what it meant on a deeper level.

I grew up in a house centred on faith. My mother is a devout Catholic, and so I've always carried an inherent belief in purpose and destiny. I've always believed that everything happens for a reason. But what I was also learning as a young man was that you must seek that purpose and destiny with your whole heart if you're going to achieve it. That was the element that was missing in my love of basketball.

One night, early in my time at Coffeyville, I sat at my desk, pulled out a sheet of paper, and made a list of what I planned to achieve. It wasn't the first time I had written about my goals. I'd done the same thing when I was in high school—get better grades, score more points, get a scholarship—but this time it was different. This list was about more than just stating my goals; it was about making myself accountable to the pursuit of them. It was about laying out a course of action to achieve them.

Run the 100 metres in under 10 seconds.

Get an NCAA scholarship.

Win the NCAA championship.

Go pro.

Win an Olympic gold medal.

Become the fastest human alive.

When I was younger, I still had time to lack confidence. But now as a young man, with this chance to prove what I was capable of, I knew I had to believe in myself. This was my last chance. And it was the only option. That meant that writing out my goals wasn't enough. Speaking it into existence meant making those goals the priority of my life.

I was determined to stay focused and true to my goals on and off the track. I knew the only person that could stop me was me. That meant early mornings on the track and late nights studying. It meant getting rid of the distractions that usually pulled me away. (Of course, it helped that there was very little to do in Coffeyville to begin with.)

My grades would be a big factor if I was going to get any attention from NCAA schools looking to recruit me. There was no messing around. That was a commitment I'd made to myself, my mother, and the school.

I'd never been much of a student. It wasn't that I found school difficult. It wasn't that hard. I just found myself bored and disinterested in class. There were too many interesting things happening beyond the classroom to distract me from those dull lessons. But at Coffeyville that changed. I sat in the front row of each of my classes. I found that I enjoyed the courses I took in college much more than I had in high school. They captured my attention.

I didn't own a laptop at the time. It was a luxury my mother and I couldn't afford. While that might have been a shocking thing to students attending a more privileged and expensive school like the University of Southern California, it was commonplace at Coffeyville. Each year, 80 to 90 percent of students at the school are on some kind of financial aid.

Because I had to use the school's computers to complete my assignments, I spent a lot of time in the library. That's where I met Coach Wood's wife, Jill. I called her Mrs. Wood. She became one of the main reasons I was able to graduate. Jill worked in the school's library and was a tutor at the student success centre. I had a difficult time with algebra and geometry, so she tutored me. We worked together for hours, making sure I understood each concept. She was incredibly patient, probably more patient than any teacher I'd had before. Sometimes she'd keep the student centre open late, just so I could keep working on an assignment or we could keep studying.

Mrs. Wood's commitment to my education was vital to helping me graduate. She helped me see my potential beyond track. She helped me see that I can achieve anything I work hard at. Looking back today, I appreciate that effort more than I was able to at the time. I wasn't the only person she worked with. It was clear that her passion was helping students achieve their goals—and I'm sure there are many Coffeyville graduates who feel the same way about her that I do.

The education I was working towards stopped being simply a means to earning a scholarship at a more prestigious school. It became a genuine interest—a new kind of passion, something I'd never experienced before.

//////

At Coffeyville, I also learned lessons about accountability that I carry with me to this day. True to his word about enforcing a commitment to education, Coach Wood called me into his office after the one day I missed class, just to confirm that I'd been sick. (I was.) There was no messing around though. Each day at Coffeyville was a lesson in accountability. If you didn't reach certain targets with your grades in the classroom, you weren't given a uniform to compete on the track. You had to earn your team sweatpants, hoodies, and T-shirts. It was as simple and strict as that.

Through my first year in the classroom, I proved to Coach Wood I was focused on getting out of Kansas and reaching the next level. He was always watching to make sure I didn't lose sight of that goal. I never did.

Outside of the classroom I trained harder than I had ever trained in my life. I spent hours on the track, working through my technique and building strength. Every meet was an opportunity to catch the attention of an NCAA recruiter.

My technique and form were still raw. I was getting better, but it was clear that most of my competitors had more formal training behind them than I had. It didn't matter. I was still a step ahead of everyone else at the finish line. In my freshman year at Coffeyville, I beat a top-ranked sprinter named Tyreek Hill, who was attending from Garden City Community College. Of course, Hill went on to pursue other passions, becoming a four-time NFL All-Pro wide receiver and a Super Bowl champion with the Kansas City Chiefs.

My success at Coffeyville quickly started to garner attention from the big NCAA programs I'd dreamed of attending. (If I found myself with any free time, I played in open runs at the basketball court. I told my friends back home that I thought I could make the varsity team and then hopefully get noticed by an NCAA recruiter. I held on to that dream as long as I could.)

I missed home, of course—I missed my mom, I missed my friends, I missed that life—but I had to leave it behind. That winter, I didn't even go home for Thanksgiving break (though I did call home often, using my iPod Touch to FaceTime my mother and friends). Despite the homesickness, I remained in Coffeyville training and working towards my goals.

And, more than ever before, I *believed* in those goals. I believed I had the power and ability to achieve them. More than that, I now had the will and commitment to work hard to make them happen.

Since that first year in Coffeyville, I've continued to live by that mantra. Speaking my goals into existence has become an exercise of action and purpose in my life. It's what pushes me to work with intention and be diligent about the plan I set out.

It's become part of who I am. It's how I view what is possible in this life. It's how I stay grounded, determined, and focused on my goals. It's how I stay positive through defeat and setbacks.

It's become about much more than what I want to achieve as an athlete. It's about the kind of man I want to be. About the kind of father I want to be—and the kind of life I want to provide for my kids. It's about the legacy I want to leave behind.

Today, when I speak to people about pursuing success in any area of life, I always return to that simple message: speak it into existence.

Say it loud. Make it real. And then set out to achieve it.

4

LET IT GO

'm very fortunate that, so far, most people who have followed my career remember only my better moments. The gold medals and podium finishes always make the highlights—but like most athletes, my career is built more on defeats than victories. That's not unique to track or to sports in general. I think that's probably the case for most people who have found some success in whatever they do.

We all lose. That's just a reality of competition. If I don't cross the finish line first, it means someone else was better than me that day. One of the lessons I've learned in my career so far is that getting beat is okay. That's not to say it's enjoyable. Anyone who has ever played pickup basketball with me will know I don't take kindly to losing. I want to be the best whenever I compete. That's just my nature.

But I've learned there is value in losing too. There is even value in losing badly. There is something to be gained from feeling so defeated and frustrated that you consider just packing it in for good. I know because I've been there several times. I don't believe I would have had the opportunity to stand on an Olympic podium without having felt the crush of disappointment many times before getting there.

The reality is that disappointment follows you regardless of how successful you are. It's inevitable. The trick is understanding how to find a positive in it. In hindsight, some of the moments I viewed as my biggest failures ended up being nothing more than a small hurdle in my career. Especially the embarrassing moments that happened early on, when I was still trying to prove to everyone, including myself, that I belonged.

In fact, the very first time I lined up beside Usain Bolt, I messed up. No one remembers this anymore, but I've never forgotten. It was August 2014. I was 19 years old and had just finished my second year at Coffeyville Community College. I was fresh into adulthood. But really, I was still a kid. I wasn't even old enough to drink yet in Kansas. I had run in my first-ever 100-metre race just two years earlier in my senior year of high school.

But there I was at the Commonwealth Games in Glasgow, Scotland, in my first season representing Canada on the senior national team. The track events took place at Hampden Park, a soccer stadium that seats more than 51,000 people. I'd never competed in front of that many spectators before. Just looking around at the sea of people that came to watch us run made me more nervous than I'd ever been.

Feeling the jitters, I managed to win my first heat in the 200 metres in 20.56 seconds. But a disappointing 20.73 in the semis fell short of advancing me to the final. I expected that to be the end for me in Glasgow.

But then our coach informed me I was running in the 4 x 100-metre relay. Oh, and on top of that, I was running anchor.

"You're going to bring it home for us," he told me. "You're going to help us get this medal."

My reaction must have betrayed my shock and concern.

"No," he said. "You can do this."

This was a huge show of faith in my ability and potential. I was honoured, but I was also nervous. I was the youngest guy in our 4 x 100 group. The only one who hadn't competed on a stage like this before. Dontae Richards-Kwok and Gavin Smellie were both veterans, several years older than me. Smellie ran the event for Canada at the 2012 London Olympics. And he'd won a bronze medal in the relay at the 2013 World Championships alongside Richards-Kwok and Aaron Brown. Brown was just a couple years older than me but had also competed in the London Olympics. These guys were already a team and I was a new, inexperienced kid.

The event was by far the biggest moment of my relatively brand new career up to that point.

On top of all that, there was Usain Bolt.

I was 13 years old when I watched Bolt win his first Olympic gold medal. I remember sitting in the basement watching highlights of his 100-metre and 200-metre races at the 2008 Beijing Games, in which he smashed the world records in both, running 9.69 and 19.30.

A few weeks later I started high school.

Bolt was world famous, the kind of athlete who transcends their sport and becomes internationally known. By 2014, there were few places in the world he could go without being instantly recognized.

I remember that night as clearly as I remember any of the best moments in my career.

The stadium was sold out. I looked around and felt overwhelmed by the sheer volume of people packed into that massive space.

"This is crazy," I thought.

But I'd managed to find some confidence ahead of the race. I told myself the usual—*you can do this, you belong here, you've got it*—forcing myself to believe it was all true. I was pumped up. I was excited.

It was short-lived. Because then I walked into the call room, where you check in before a race. And there was Usain Bolt. The nerves flooded back. I specifically remember noticing how tall he was. He was a giant among us.

"Shoot. I'm about to race against him?" I thought.

This was the first time I'd ever lined up beside him. A year after the Beijing Olympics, Bolt broke his own records in both events, running 9.58 and 19.19 (both of which still stand).

Our team was told we would race in lane six. Jamaica was in lane five. Bolt, of course, would run anchor for a team that set the world record in the relay two years earlier, with a time of 36.84.

In the call room I stripped off my sweats and an official stuck my number on my bib. The room was quiet. Everyone was in their zone, getting prepared for the race. I could feel my nerves spinning. It grew worse when we were instructed to head out to the track. As we walked out in front of more than 51,000 fans, the noise inside the open-air stadium erupted. It was overwhelming. I'd never heard a crowd that loud before. It was a jarring contrast from the silent anticipation just moments before. The white lights around the oval sparkled against a dark blue sky, casting reflections in the puddles of water that pooled around the track after a day of rain.

Our team huddled together before the race, trying to hype ourselves up as much as possible.

"All right guys! Let's bring it home," one of them said. I was too nervous to remember who.

"Let's get this medal!" said another.

"Okay, cool," I said—or something half-convincing like that.

I felt my entire body tingling. The nerves were overwhelming now.

"Damn . . . okay," I said to myself. "Just focus. Take some deep breaths. I'll be all right."

As the stadium announcer called out each of the teams, Bolt dropped into his famous thunderbolt stance, pointing upwards, and the crowd went wild. He blew them a kiss, forming peace signs with his fingers, nodding with his fastest-in-the-world confidence.

In the lane beside him, my legs wobbled as I tried to shake the jitters out.

Just focus . . . Deep breaths.

One hundred metres away, the race was about to begin.

"On your marks," the starter called.

"Set."

And the gun cracked. The stadium, somehow, got even louder as the race barrelled around the track towards me.

We did well through the first 200, sitting second beside Jamaica. Then we fell behind a bit on the corner, dropping slightly back behind South Africa and England. But I wouldn't see any of that until afterwards, when I'd watch this race over and over, trying to figure out what happened next.

I started to move as soon as Bolt took off beside me. After a few strides I reached back expecting to feel the baton hit my left hand. But there was nothing but air. I glanced back and saw Dontae several strides behind me, moving the baton to his right hand, knowing our chance was blown. I looked up to the clouds as he ran past me and all the others running anchor rushed to the finish line.

I've watched the video hundreds of times. What was I thinking? I'd lost my nerve and my focus—and left early. I was out of sync with my teammate. The mistake meant we went from being in contention for a medal to getting a DNF (did not finish) in the final. This was the biggest stage I'd had the chance to compete on and I'd blown it brutally. I'd never felt so humiliated in my life. I didn't even clutch the baton in my hand. It was garbage.

I felt so bad. While Bolt and his teammates celebrated another victory, this time setting a Commonwealth Games record, my teammates tried to console me on the track. But I knew they were just as disappointed as I was. This was much worse than losing an individual race. I'd let everyone down, while representing my country.

This is still pretty fresh. Just revisiting the memory makes me wince.

After the race we got on the bus and rode in silence back to the athletes' village, where we were staying together in a quad-style dorm. It was late and everyone was exhausted. But I didn't go back to our room. I couldn't face the guys; I couldn't even face myself.

I just didn't want to be around anybody because I thought everyone would be mad at me. I went to find something to eat by myself and then found a bench outside to sit on alone. Whenever I need to reflect, I listen to music. It helps me escape. I drown out the world around me and settle into my thoughts.

I can't recall what music I listened to that night. The songs didn't even matter. I was distraught, certain this was the end of my career. I was convinced I didn't have what it took to be an elite sprinter. It felt like everything was about to fall apart, including any shot I had at making it to a World Championship or the Olympics. I just didn't think I could handle the pressure.

"Damn, I don't know if I want to do this," I thought. I felt it in my heart. "This is bad."

I was going to quit.

"I don't want to have this feeling again."

No one knew where I'd gone. I hadn't told any of my teammates that I wouldn't be back after dinner, but I figured they wouldn't care much. I was sure they were mad at me. The new guy had just screwed up their chance at winning a medal. I was scared to face them.

I don't even remember how long I was gone, but sometime in the middle of the night I snuck back into the dorm. Everyone was sleeping when I got back, which is what I was hoping for. I hardly slept that night. I kept running through that moment over and over again in my mind.

When I woke up the next morning, I had to face what I'd been trying to avoid. The guys were already up. But to my surprise, they didn't seem angry at all. They were concerned.

"We were worried about you, man."

"You were gone all night. Are you okay?"

They'd worried that something happened to me because I

hadn't come back. I told them I was trying to stay away because I'd ruined the race for everyone. They shot that down right away.

"It's all good, man. Don't worry about it."

"It's okay—you're young."

"We'll get it right the next time," I remember the guys telling me.

"Stuff happens. We'll get it next time."

"Keep your head up."

Everyone was so kind. The relief was overwhelming.

"You've got years ahead of you."

"You're young. So don't let that be a defining moment in your career."

I started to feel better right away. I guess I needed that. It made me feel good to know they had my back.

We spoke about putting the race in the back of our minds. We decided it was better to just not talk about it. That was the past now. It was time to move forward and get ready for the next year.

It's amazing how much a kind word or gesture can mean to someone who has worked themselves up to feeling like everything is falling apart. These guys were all more experienced than I was. They'd been through disappointment before. They'd learned how to get through those moments and to improve because of them, rather than let the disappointment destroy you.

"I'm good," I told them. "I'm good. I'm all right."

And I was.

It was the last race of the season. But it wasn't going to be the last race of my career. I was still shaken by what had happened, but I had time to learn from it now. It was a few months before I got back out there in a race again. Every moment I spent training was about trying to build my confidence. More than ever, I was determined to become one of the best. I wanted to make sure that what happened at the Commonwealth Games never happened to me again.

I used it as fuel. I told myself that the next time I stepped out there on the line, I was going to get it right. I wasn't going to let this happen again. I wouldn't freak out; I wouldn't let my nerves defeat me. I'd learn to love the crowd, to thrive in the noise and excitement.

When I got to my next big competition, there were no nerves. I don't know what happened. It was like I just flipped a switch. I was locked in. I was ready. I'd been through the worst and my career survived.

A month later, I'd be attending the University of Southern California on a full athletic scholarship. A year later, I'd be the NCAA champion in both the 100 and 200 metres. And that would be just the beginning of so much more.

But back then, I couldn't see that. Back then, I'd been ready to hang up my spikes and quit.

It took the graciousness and wisdom of my teammates to keep me going. Even though I can still remember that race like it was yesterday, it's become something that I can smile about today. Few moments have helped me the way that embarrassing night did. Now I can see it was something that was bound to happen. It was something I needed to go through to take care of the insecurity and doubt I carried, unsure of myself as I arrived at the top level of my sport.

There were many disappointments to come in my career. And don't get me wrong, they still affected me. I was still susceptible to self-doubt. But I was better prepared to use that disappointment to propel me forward. The kindness of my older teammates in Glasgow helped me learn a valuable lesson about how we frame defeat, and how we can better use it to find future success.

To me, the key message is that *it's in the past*. Let it go. Worry about the present—and then worry about the future. But don't go back to the past. Don't dwell on that moment, unless you're revisiting what you can learn from it. It happened for a reason. Now you can move on and be better than that.

5

CHASE WINS, NOT RECORDS

Early in my life I learned that admiring my heroes wasn't enough. Growing up, I adored basketball players like Michael Jordan and Kobe Bryant. I consumed whatever information I could find about them. I read articles and books. I watched interviews and documentaries. I was obsessed with learning everything I could about what made them great. I wanted to learn what they knew. How they achieved their success.

From guys like Kobe and Jordan, I learned that if you want to be the best, you need to beat the best. That means more than just saying it. It means believing it and seeking it with everything you have. It means seeing the person who sits on the throne and knowing you belong there too.

I've always carried much more swagger on a basketball court than I did on a track. (You can ask any of the friends I still play pickup with today.) That's probably because I came to sprinting later than most and felt like I was catching up. But as I gained confidence, I also gained perspective.

I knew if I wanted to be the best, there was only one person I had to catch.

To the version of me that watched Usain Bolt win double gold at the Beijing Olympics in 2008, the idea of one day surpassing him would have seemed crazy. To the version of me that stood beside him on the line at the Commonwealth Games in Glasgow six years later, it still seemed impossible. But at the Rio Olympics in 2016, I believed I could win. Over those two years, something changed in me. I realized that if I was going to be the best, I had to truly believe I could.

A lot had happened to build that confidence since my embarrassing mistake in the 4 x 100. I'd become the NCAA champion in both the 100 and 200 metres. I'd also won double gold in both events at the Pan American Games in Toronto. In front of my friends and family, where I grew up, I became the first Canadian to run sub-20 in the 200 metres. At the Pan Ams, I set a Canadian record over 200 metres of 19.88 seconds (beating my previous record of 20.03).

By that point, I was only three years into my career as a runner. I'd learned a lot about myself and what I was capable of in those few years. I'd realized I was one of the fastest in the world—and more importantly, that I could be faster still.

A month later I travelled to Beijing for my first-ever World Championships. It was by far the biggest stage of my career to that point.

I lined up against Bolt in the 100-metre semifinals feeling much more confident in myself than I had a year earlier. Bolt stumbled off the start in our race and needed to give everything he had to catch us. We both clocked 9.96, with him a fraction ahead. I couldn't believe I'd been so close.

Bolt took gold in the final, barely edging out Justin Gatlin, who took silver. I was as astonished as anyone when I ran a personal best 9.92, tying Trayvon Bromell for the bronze medal. I was so happy for Trayvon, who is the same age as me and was a rising star for the United States, and at the time, the world junior record holder in the 100 metres. Finishing off the season by running a personal best, after the pressure of the NCAA championships and the Pan Am Games, was an incredible feeling. I was so proud of that bronze medal.

I draped myself in a Canadian flag and smiled as wide as ever. A television reporter asked what I had to say. I shook my head.

"I'm just so happy to be here right now," I said. "To race against these guys in the final and to get myself a bronze medal. The season couldn't have ended the way it has—"

I started laughing. I was so excited I couldn't gather my thoughts. I was trying to say that the season couldn't have ended any better, but I just couldn't get the words out.

"I'm speechless," I said.

A moment later, Bolt interrupted the live interview.

"Sorry," he said to the interviewer. He put his arm around me and gave me a quick hug.

"Congrats, man," he said.

To me.

It was unbelievable!

"Did you even know who he was when the season started?" the interviewer asked Bolt.

"To tell you the truth, no," Bolt said, with his arm on my shoulder. I shook my head, laughing, knowing he was telling the truth.

"Great job, that's all I can say," he said, shaking my hand. "Well done. Well done, man."

"So how about that? How does that feel?" the interviewer asked as Bolt walked away, wrapped in the Jamaican flag.

This time I found the words:

"To be respected by Usain Bolt, the king, the greatest of all time in the world, I'm so happy right now," I said.

The GOAT.

Without a doubt, Bolt was the fastest man alive. The fastest to have ever lived. And he was congratulating *me*. To that point, this was the craziest moment of my life. I was elated. I was humbled just standing next to him.

But I was also catching up.

I knew I was improving; I knew I was getting closer. The impossible didn't seem quite so far away anymore.

That fall I signed my first endorsement contract with Puma, which was a life-changing moment for me and my family.

Of course, Bolt was also a Puma athlete. The fact that he was heading into his final Olympics in Rio only added to the narrative that I was in line to take his throne. The media loved the connection that Bolt and I seemed to share, on the track and in media interviews. They talked about it being a "bromance," which was a little over the top. There was a camaraderie—a kind of big brother, little brother storyline. And as a rising star in the sport, it appeared as though I was on the verge of taking the baton from Bolt. That motivated me.

I'd come a long way from coming undone in Glasgow. I'd learned so much about myself and my ability. I knew more about my strengths and my weaknesses. I knew more about my competitors. I knew how to improve and was confident I would. It wasn't a matter of if—it was a matter of when.

When would I stand on the podium as the fastest in the world?

I want to be careful here, because it's easy for confidence to be confused with arrogance. The excitement I carried when I won my very first medal at a World Championships was real. I was genuinely astonished to find myself in that moment—just as I had been at the Pan Am Games earlier that summer and the NCAA championships before that. I was watching a dream come true. I was living it. The awe I felt for Bolt was authentic. It was like one of my basketball idols—Kobe or Jordan—coming up and congratulating me on my success. Unimaginable. When I say I was humbled, I genuinely mean that.

But by that point in my career, I knew I owed it to myself to not be anchored in that humility. I needed to believe in myself the way the athletes I aspired to be like did. I'd developed the work ethic. I just needed the mentality.

As an athlete, as a competitor, I always wanted to be like Bolt. To win an Olympic gold medal, to be a crowd favourite, to run in that spotlight. And so that was how I looked at him: I wanted to find out the secrets of what made him great.

I understand now that this is a fundamental part of striving to be the best. You have to find out what makes your idols extraordinary, and you have to learn from that wisdom. But you also need to truly believe you can be extraordinary too. You need to chase your heroes—and believe you can catch them.

For me, running alongside Bolt wasn't enough. Receiving his public praise, as honoured as I was, wasn't enough.

I wanted to beat him. I believed I could beat him. I had to believe that, otherwise what was I trying to accomplish?

As my first Olympics neared the following summer, I continued to work with that goal in mind.

Despite the success I'd had, I was still relatively unknown outside of the world of track. Most Canadians hadn't heard of me before Rio. But my competitors were aware of what I could do. I'd earned their respect. I'd gone from being the guy who was just trying to beat everyone to being the guy with the target on his back. Now everyone was trying to beat me. I couldn't let that happen. I had to stay on top in every race.

I didn't want to put too much pressure on myself heading to Rio. Expectation is important, but it can become a distraction if you let it. There is a balance to the pressure you want to put on yourself. But I knew I was capable of doing something special if I put my mind to it.

Before Rio, I told the press I planned to win three medals at the Olympics, which was viewed as brash by some, considering that Athletics Canada had set a goal of winning two or three medals for the entire team. I was asked about Bolt constantly leading up to the Games. The media loved the storyline of me trying to surpass Bolt. I played into it. He'd announced that these would be his last Olympics just before the Games began. If there was ever going to be a time to catch him, this was it.

"I never thought I'd be able to run as fast as him because you know—that's crazy," I told the *Globe and Mail* before the Olympics. "But now that I've run under 10 seconds, I feel that I can."

In Rio, the press continued to drive a storyline about the perceived bond between me and Bolt. During a press conference before the 100-metre event, Bolt told the room that I reminded him of a younger version of himself.

"It's always good to see the younger guys coming up and showing that they're ready to take over and running fast times and keeping the sport on a high," he said. "So for me, it's good on all fronts."

It was kind. But I wasn't there to be Bolt's buddy. And he wasn't interested in being mine. We were both there with the same goal in mind.

I lined up beside Bolt in the 100-metre final. I was in lane seven; he was in lane six. At 21 years old, I was the youngest on the line. Everything that had come before was leading up to this moment.

I looked up after I crossed the line, running the 100 metres faster than I'd ever run it before: 9.91 seconds. A personal best. My name flashed third. Bronze. I'd done it. I was an Olympic medallist. I'd finished a fraction behind Justin Gatlin, who took silver, and Bolt, who won his third straight gold.

He gave me another compliment after the race:

"For me, De Grasse has shown he is ready," he told the Canadian Press. "He's done it back-to-back from last year. So we know the future of the sport is in good hands."

There wasn't much time to enjoy the moment. The next day, heats for the 200-metre race began. It was the event that both Bolt and I preferred, even though he'd run it sparingly over the past year. I felt like I had an even better chance of pushing him here than I had in the 100. After advancing through our preliminary heats, Bolt and I lined up beside each other again in the 200-metre semifinals.

I sometimes get asked how it felt racing against Bolt with our significant height difference. Usain is 6-foot-5 and I'm a generous 5-foot-10. But the answer I give is always the same: when I stepped onto the track in Rio, I felt 10 feet tall.

Before the race, my coach, Stuart McMillan, and I spoke about the best strategy to take in the semis. We were confident I could make the final. That was the expectation. Anything less would have been disappointing. But we also knew Bolt was likely to lead the pack, as he usually did. Instead of letting Bolt cruise to an easy first-place finish in the semis, we decided I should push him at the line as much as possible, not letting up the way sprinters often do once they've established a position that will secure a spot in the final. Winning the heat didn't mean much on paper, but this was Bolt's final Olympics. If I could force him to use an extra burst of energy in the semifinals, we figured, it just might take enough gas out of him for the final. Any extra edge could be a difference maker when it came to standing on the podium.

Bolt was a step ahead as we turned the corner into the final stretch. I knew I was in position to qualify, but I kept pushing. The final stretch was my strength—and this was my chance to make Bolt sweat. With about 30 metres to go, I looked over at him, just ahead, and found another gear. The move surprised Bolt and he had to push to edge out what had looked like an easy win for him. We were looking right at each other before crossing the line, both smiling. Usain wagged his finger at me.

I finished two one-hundredths of a second behind him. My 19.80 was a new personal record, beating the previous Canadian record that I held.

As Bolt slowed down he wore a kind of astonished, amused

grin. I went over and he gave me a side-hug, putting his arm on my shoulder.

The broadcasters loved it. So did viewers around the world—and especially back home in Canada.

"This brotherhood continues," one CBC commentator said.

The push to win in the semifinals, when most people would have let up, was a bold statement about how I viewed myself and what I was capable of. If I was going to stand beside the greatest sprinter in history, I was going to give it everything I had.

Some noted the smile on my face as I crossed the line. They wondered if I was sending a message that I had a lot more left. That it was a sign I was supremely confident, but also extremely relaxed. That I had no fear—that I truly believed I could beat Bolt.

I was smiling because I *had* almost beaten Bolt. I was smiling because I was exhausted. I'd given everything I had and nearly caught the GOAT. I was smiling because I loved every second of it.

Later, Bolt told reporters he chastised me for pushing so hard in the semis.

"It's just one of those things," he said. "He's young, so . . ." Bolt may have been smiling but he was doing that while wagging his finger at me, like *Chill out, dude.*

But overall, people made a much bigger deal of it than it was. The storyline was intriguing and fun—it was good for the sport—but I don't believe there was any real animosity. Of course, my strategy of trying to burn out his energy in the semifinals didn't work. Bolt won his third straight Olympic gold medal in the final the next day. I led the pack behind him, chasing greatness.

I took silver, my second-ever Olympic medal. It was the first medal a Canadian had won in the event since Percy Williams won gold in 1928. It was a huge moment for me. But to this day, people mostly remember the semis and the smile Bolt and I shared as we crossed the line, matching stride for stride.

At the World Championships in London a year later, Bolt injured his hamstring running anchor for Jamaica in the relay. He fell to the track with about 50 metres to go as the other sprinters passed him. His teammates gathered around him, helping him up. Bolt brushed off the support of a wheelchair and limped towards the finish line. He crossed it as the undisputed champion in the sport—carrying both the 100- and 200-metre world records, along with eight Olympic gold medals. A legacy that will likely never be challenged.

If there was a bromance between us, it fizzled after Rio. There was no animosity. Our relationship was just never what the media made it. Our paths didn't cross very often, and I never really spoke with him beyond the Rio Olympics.

To this day, I'm asked about Bolt all the time. Looking back, I can see that my experience with him taught me a lesson about admiring greatness, respecting it—but also believing you can achieve it.

Several years later when I won the Olympic gold medal that I dreamed of, one of the most memorable messages I received was a brief voice memo sent to me via Instagram from Bolt.

It was simple and sweet.

"Yo bro-ski! Congrats, congrats on the win, boss," he said. "You deserve it. You've been through a hell of a lot. Keep your head up—and keep pushing. All right?"

"Haha, Respect bro," I typed back. "Appreciate it. 🙏🐐"

And I mean that respect. Bolt remains the GOAT. But I'm not trying to follow his footsteps.

I'm forging my own path.

When you think about the greats in a sport like basketball, Kobe Bryant and LeBron James are two of the best ever. But when they competed, they weren't trying to do the same thing—aside from winning. They didn't think about scoring 50 points in a game. They thought about how to win the game, and the 50 points came if that's what it took. There is an important distinction there. You'll never see a great player celebrate scoring 50 points if they lost the game. Guys like Bryant and LeBron would only think about what they needed to do to win—and that's it. That was the only objective that mattered. It wasn't a scoring title, or the league MVP. Those accolades would come as the by-product of winning, but they were always secondary.

Today, LeBron is completing his own legacy, not chasing the legacy of Kobe or Michael Jordan, even though the media and fans love to make comparisons. In the end, each of them took their own path to greatness.

That's how I think about competition too. Some people chase the clock, but I just want to win.

Early in my career I was often asked if I was going to be the next Bolt. I understood why, but that was never my goal. I didn't want to be the next Usain Bolt; I was the first Andre De Grasse. I just wanted to be myself. I didn't want to chase him. Of course, in a way, Bolt's 100-metre world record of 9.58 and his 200-metre world record of 19.19 set the standard we all dream of beating. But it's not like Bolt ran those times every day.

Everyone who steps on the track to compete at this level only runs their fastest time once. We can set a personal best one day and then be a tenth of a second slower the next time we run, which doesn't seem like a lot to most people, but it's a big difference in the sport. When you're competing for fractions of a second, you can't run your best every time you step on the track. It's a constant battle to push past your best.

I always aim to run a personal best, but it's impossible to do that every race. I might run a personal best once a season, or even once every two seasons. The more important, attainable goal is to be consistent. I want to run close to my personal best every time I compete. I've medalled in every Olympic and World Championship final I've competed in, which is more important to me than breaking records.

One day soon, I hope to set another personal best. One day, my personal best could be a world record. But that's an outcome I'm not worried about. Bolt is not the target when I stand on the line. When I get set, I'm not thinking about the world record or even my personal record. I'm thinking about running the fastest I can in that moment and beating everyone else beside me to the finish line. I'm thinking about executing to get the win.

At the Tokyo Olympics, I set out to win gold in the 200 metres. In achieving that goal, I broke the Canadian record and set another personal best.

I think that's how we should view competition in any area of life where we are trying to hit our goals and be the best we can be. Set out to achieve your goals each day. End each day knowing you've racked up another win in whichever areas of life you hope to achieve success. Set lofty goals in your life, but know you will never reach them without those wins each day. Celebrate those victories, and then stay determined to keep earning them. If you stay focused on those efforts, success will follow.

6

THE RESPONSIBILITY OF SUCCESS

Those who know me well know I'm an introvert in public settings. With my friends, I'm myself. I'm outgoing. I have fun. I feel free to relax. My friends are always asking me to be like that when I'm out in public, but I find it very difficult. I love to meet people, to pose for photographs, sign autographs, and have conversations with strangers. But I'm always reserved. I need to see my surroundings and get to know people. I need to see what *their* vibes are like before I reveal mine.

I wasn't aware of how shy I can be before people started to recognize me on the street. Before that, I didn't have to consider what people's motivations or intentions were for wanting to get close to me. Of course, most people are genuine and kind. Most people just want to say hello and be acknowledged back. But being in the public eye has taught me to read people in a way I didn't before. I've found I need to be guarded while I figure out whether I can trust people and be myself. I've learned to let other people show their real personality before I let them see mine. I guess it's kind of like a "see how they are" approach. I don't know if that's a good thing or a bad thing. Maybe I should show more of myself, like my friends always bug me about. Or maybe I'm right to be cautious. Either way, it's one of the many things I had to adjust to when I first reached a level of fame I'd never anticipated.

I can still remember the first time I felt "famous." It was a very weird feeling and still is. After I returned to Toronto from the Rio Olympics in 2016 with three Olympic medals, my friends started to notice that people seemed to be looking in our direction wherever we went.

This started to happen occasionally after the Pan American Games in Toronto in 2015, where I think I kind of surprised everyone (including myself) by winning gold in the 100- and 200-metre races. It grew after the World Championships in Beijing later that summer when I took bronze in the 100 metres and was part of the team that won bronze in the 100-metre relay. But then I started my second year at the University of Southern California (USC) on the scholarship I'd dreamt of getting, and I spent most of the year outside of Canada. I knew some people were aware of who I was back home now. But I don't think most people would have recognized me on the street.

After Rio, everything changed. It was a whole different level. Track fans followed those earlier successes, but everybody pays attention to the Olympics.

At least that's what it seemed like: everybody was watching.

Random people would stop me to say hello and offer congratulations—and ask for an autograph or photo. It was nice, but it was sudden. Some people wanted to talk longer than others, which trapped me in a lot of conversations I didn't know how to get out of. It meant that my friends or whatever family members I was with were stuck waiting for me. I had a lot to learn.

That was when I first started receiving messages on my Instagram account from people with blue checks, meaning they were verified celebrities. I already had a blue check at the time, but this was different—these were A-list people.

"Oh, wow," I remember thinking. "This is cool. "

I was about to turn 22 years old at the time, and in many ways I was still a kid. I was just out of my college phase, that time in life when you're moving from relatively carefree life as a teen into the challenges and responsibilities of being an independent person. I had to learn those lessons quickly when I left for Coffeyville and then USC—as I became an elite athlete, training constantly to run against the fastest in the world. It was a steep learning curve.

So whenever I returned home and had a chance to hang with my closest friends, the guys who'd been with me since the start of high school, it was a nice break from all of that. I wanted to let loose and be myself. I wanted to be the real me, who only they knew. It wasn't that we'd get into trouble—it was more about being relaxed and unguarded. Listening to music, going out—being young. But I had to be very careful now. I had a responsibility as a Canadian Olympian to represent the country, just as I'd had a responsibility to USC and the NCAA as a student-athlete on a full scholarship. Every action I took carried potential consequences. Every fan I interacted with, every random person I crossed paths with, every cellphone that caught me on video—every move I made in a public place was a reflection not only of myself but also of what I now represented.

Being recognized was one of the most unexpected results of the success I had after the Rio Olympics, but it forced me to learn a valuable lesson about how I carry myself. Just as there is a responsibility to compete within the rules, there is a duty that comes with the attention of being an ambassador for the sport. There is an expectation that I be a role model to the young people who found inspiration in watching me run. I'm honoured by the fact that anyone would consider me a role model, and I believe I need to continue to earn that position every day.

With that in mind, I always want to be the best version of myself wherever I am. When I interact with fans, I can't have an off moment. Even if I'm having a bad day, I need to make sure I'm presenting a version of myself that comes off as appealing and genuine. Don't get me wrong—most of the time, I don't have a problem with that. I'm always honoured that fans want to talk to me, but we all have down days. I had to learn to smile and engage with strangers—to think of every situation as a professional moment.

It was a lot to take on, and I'd be lying if it didn't cause me some anxiety at the start. I tried to go with the flow. But I became way more aware of my surroundings than I'd ever been before.

The regulations I need to follow just to be allowed to compete are like a full-time job on their own. To make sure I am available to be drug tested at any given time, I have to update my location every day. It's a modern process: you log into an app, note where you will be sleeping that night and where you can be found the following day for a specific time window, during which officials can randomly show up to test you.

The official, working on behalf of the Athletics Integrity Unit, isn't going to come every day—but if you forget to update your location and they show up at the last address you entered, that's a strike against you. If you get three strikes you can get suspended from competition for anywhere from one to three years, depending on the situation.

It might sound simple, but in the midst of a busy life, training, travelling to compete, travelling to events, and commercial shoots for brands—on top of being a father with a house full of kids—it's a small detail that can be easily forgotten. When I was a bit younger, it meant that being out at a party or over at my girlfriend's house had to be logged. If I just lost track of time, it didn't matter.

In fact, it's something I've forgotten a few times, and it's created a lot of anxiety for my management team.

I've reached two strikes before.

I was absolutely terrified for a month, waiting for the 12-month cycle to end so the strikes would reset. I'd get constant texts and calls from my marketing agent Brian Levine and my track agent Paul Doyle, checking in to make sure I was where my app indicated. Everyone was on high alert.

That was a tense month—just because of a stupid app.

But at the same time, I understand it's necessary. It's about maintaining the integrity of our sport. It's about taking personal responsibility for that integrity every day.

//////

Looking back on that time in my life, it's clear that this is when I first took that full step into adulthood. I wasn't a father yet. And I was still just starting the journey of my career. But I gained a sense of responsibility I've carried ever since. It woke me up to the enormous privilege I have to do what I do. It changed my perspective.

I know that I'm lucky to have the career that I do. People rarely get the chance to do this—to represent their country. In track, only three people from your country can compete per event. I try to keep that in mind whenever I start to feel overwhelmed or discouraged. I'm fortunate. I'm one of the few. And with that privilege comes responsibility.

But there are some downsides that come with fame. Every once in a while, a fan will go a bit too far and make public moments awkward. There are demands on my time I need to balance out. I get a lot of requests, almost daily, to attend and speak at events. They are often events I want to take part in—for schools, charity groups, and sponsors. I'm always honoured by a request. It still amazes me that people want to meet me, let alone hear what I have to say. I try my best to take part in everything I reasonably am able to. But it can be overwhelming. Over the years I've had to learn how to say "no." I've learned I can't please everyone, and that's okay.

I also had to learn to deal with unexpected negativity. I learned that people will say things about you online, trying to tear down what you've worked hard to achieve. I learned that sometimes people will shout those things at you in the street. While most of the interactions I had after Rio were positive, I also had people let me know they felt that I suck at what I do—that my medals were a fluke and that I was overrated. I learned to laugh those ones off.

I learned that whether the feedback is positive or negative, you can't get too caught up in the noise, or it will become a distraction to what you are working to achieve.

I've forgotten about most of the negative things people have said about me. And even though I didn't want to rest on the positive feedback I received from fans, it has absolutely been a life-changing experience. I never forgot those comments. You'd hear stories from people about how watching me run had been an inspiration and motivation in their life. I was told by one fan that they had watched me race while lying in a hospital bed. I was told about people who watched with loved ones who are no longer around—a happy memory they now cherish, after losing them. I was told by complete strangers that those brief seconds when I was barrelling down a track made them proud and that I'd made the *country* proud.

Those are the kinds of stories I carry with me as motivation. They are the stories that keep me moving on days when I feel exhausted. They are what give me strength as I battle through an injury or as I face another disappointing result. Those are the stories that remind me I've got to keep doing this—I've got to keep going—I've got to keep making those people proud.

Early in my career, that success created a new pressure I hadn't experienced before. The other side of making people proud when you succeed is disappointing them when you don't. So as much as I wanted Canadians to feel pride in my success, I felt the weight of those expectations on my shoulders. I didn't want to let anyone down. I wanted to keep making people proud of me. I was already motivated by my own goals, but now it felt like I had an obligation to the fans who had shown me so much love and support.

Success became a burden, for a time. As I was still learning to become the best athlete I could be on the track, I was also learning to prepare myself for the challenges that arise when you actually do achieve what you set out to accomplish. It's very rare to find someone who is competitive enough to have achieved their goals suddenly stop trying to succeed. Once we reach one goal, our measure of success changes.

From the moment I won my first race, I craved that high. I just wanted to keep going and keep pushing. To get faster and faster. That's competition and drive. That's what it takes to be a champion. But distraction comes with the outside expectations. Winning those medals in Rio put more attention on me—and on the fact I hadn't yet won an Olympic gold. At least that's how I felt. If I was going to make people proud, I had to do better than I'd done before.

I don't want to suggest that meeting those expectations was my only motivation. More than anything, I was still driven to reach my own goals and to make my family and friends, the people who stood by me through everything, proud. I wanted to honour them because of the love they'd given and the sacrifices they'd made so I could achieve these dreams. But outside pressure and noise did get to me. At some point the praise and the doubt can all blend together and become a hindrance.

I had to learn that lesson very early on. This is where my tendency to be an introvert became an effective tool. I learned to look inward and to compartmentalize. I learned that in the same way I find it hard to be myself around people before I get to know them, I also need to keep some distance from the expectations those people have of me. I can't always win, but I won't always lose. What matters is that I'm fine with that and the people I love are fine with that. What matters is that those victories and defeats are all part of a process—*my process*—towards achieving *my* goals.

I focused on what I was able to control. As my world got bigger, I made the world around me smaller. I'd stay in my own little bubble. I learned to avoid distractions like social media and whatever people are saying online. I surrounded myself with people I love and respect. People, like my mother and my family and friends, who remind me that no matter what happens, they'll always love me. They'd tell me to "Go out there and be you—and make it happen." I listened to their voices, their encouragement, their concerns, knowing they were looking out for my best interests.

In the years after Rio, I'd face several challenges in which being able to drown out the noise became essential. Through the many defeats that followed on the way to reaching my goals, I had to remind myself to live with the results as they came. Whatever happened, I knew that at the end of the day, I'd put in the hard work. I'd done everything possible to succeed. I was still fuelled by the positive messages I received from people I didn't know. It still inspired and motivated me. But I wouldn't let it add pressure to the expectations I already carried for myself. I wasn't interested in the noise, but others often brought my attention to articles or social media comments that questioned my ability. Especially during my long recovery from my hamstring injury, there were people who questioned whether I'd reached my peak. People in my inner circle are very protective of me, which I appreciate. I know their intention is in the right place. But I told them to not pay any attention to the noise. I couldn't let it take control over me. I wasn't going to let that doubt find a place in my mind.

I learned to find a balance between the outside expectations and the criticism that follow success—and to turn both into positive motivation.

7

MAMA'S BOY

I was always a mama's boy growing up.

I'm incredibly lucky to have a mother who is always there for me. She worked to make sure I had whatever I needed when I was young. And even now, if I ever ask her to do something, she's there. Right away.

I've learned how necessary it is to appreciate the people in your life who have given you a path to pursue your dreams. It's very rare for someone to achieve excellence on their own. There are people who support and guide you. People who make the impossible possible.

Few people have taught me as much or inspired me more than my mother, Beverley De Grasse. Today, I'm still learning lessons about life by reflecting on everything she's given me.

When I was young, it was just me and my mom. I was her only child, so it was just the two of us, mother and son.

I was a happy kid—but also a hyper kid. My mom used to think

I might have attention-deficit disorder. (I appreciate her even more now, because I can see how much energy it takes to raise my own kids. They are basically jumping off the walls non-stop.) As a single mother, she bore all the responsibility for raising me. I didn't make it easy—I could throw temper tantrums with the best of them. Mom had to be strict at times. We operated on a one-strike policy, where most kids got three. If I acted up at the mall, for example, we just left. It was tough love, but it was *always* love. She was an early childhood educator, so she was already an expert. There wasn't much I could get past her.

When I was four, my mother went back to college to complete her certification in early childhood education (a field she had worked in back in Trinidad before coming to Canada). She somehow found a way to make our world work while she juggled college, work, and raising me. We were fortunate that she had a lot of family around—two brothers and two sisters—which is why I think family is something I've always valued. I spent a lot of time at my aunt's house while Mom was at school. There was a lot of love raising me.

Our place was always busy, even though it was just Mom and me living there. Her brothers and sisters all had a lot of kids, so I was surrounded by cousins. We were all around the same age. We had all kinds of house parties, dinners, and holidays. Mom always cooked—macaroni and cheese, roti, curry chicken. I loved my mother's cooking. I still do. Whenever I come back to visit her, the first thing I ask is for her to make me a plate. I never want to eat out when I'm at home. My mom's cooking is just too good to miss out on.

Our Caribbean heritage has always been important to us. There was always calypso or soca music playing in our house.

We went to Caribana every year, all the way up to my last year of high school. Mom always went all out for the celebration in downtown Toronto. We'd also travel to Trinidad when I was young to visit my mother's family every February for Carnival, which was always fun. My mom's father passed away before I was born, but my grandmother still lived there. My mom had two brothers and a sister who lived there too.

Mom worked hard and she worked a lot. When she went back to school, she'd attend class all day and then pick me up from daycare, drive me to her brother's house, and then leave for her part-time job at a mail-sorting company in the evenings. After her shift, she'd pick me up and take me home to go to bed. On the weekends she often worked at a hair salon.

She always had multiple jobs, but somehow she also found a way to make sure she was there for me. After she received her college certification, her primary job was at a daycare centre. During March break when I was in elementary school, she would bring me with her to the daycare so she and the other teachers could keep an eye on me. That was her day job, but she'd continue to work part time in the evenings and on the weekends throughout my childhood.

From my boyhood perspective, I knew only that she would work one job during the day—and then she would come home and leave to do another job or attend class at night and on the weekends. Of course, I didn't realize how much she was doing and how hard she was working back then. You don't realize that as a kid. It was just what my mom did. I didn't know it was abnormal or what the sacrifice meant.

I was born in Scarborough, on the eastern edge of Toronto.

We lived in a basement apartment near Woodside Mall, close to Brimley Road and Finch Avenue East. It was a busy area, and my mother dreamed of moving us to a place where I could have the space and freedom to be a kid without her having to worry about me. When I was in the second grade we moved to Markham, a suburb just north of Scarborough. Mom had saved up enough money to get a mortgage on a semi-detached three-bedroom house. That's the place I remember most from my youth. I thought it was enormous as a kid. I loved it so much. It was a nice house from an eight-year-old kid's perspective, but as you get older you realize it was actually pretty small.

But it was *our* house, in a much more suburban neighbourhood. A lot of people were moving there at the time. We lived on Risebrough Circuit, which was a street lined with modest beige and pink brick homes with single-car garages, typical of Toronto's suburbs that expanded through the '80s and '90s. The new street opened a whole new world for me.

Our place was right next to Risebrough Park, and there were three elementary schools nearby. That meant there was plenty of space to play, which was a lot different from our neighbourhood at Brimley and Finch. There was a basketball court, a soccer field, and a baseball diamond around the corner. For a hyperactive kid, that meant hours outside burning energy. It also opened so many opportunities for me and allowed my passion for sports to flourish.

Sports were the only outlet that could tire me out, so my mom kept me busy. She signed me up for every sport possible by the time I was four years old: soccer, baseball, basketball—anything to tire me out. I even played hockey for a time, but I didn't want to learn how to skate. But I did play street hockey. I still have a scar above my eye from when one of my friends on my street took a slapshot and smacked me right in the face. I had to go to the hospital to get stitches. I didn't play much hockey after that—I was a bit traumatized. Maybe it's why I gravitated to soccer, baseball, and basketball.

In Scarborough I couldn't do all that. I wasn't able to go outside by myself. And I didn't know many kids I could just go outside and play with anyway.

Away from those busy streets, I now had a safe place to meet other kids. And there were so many of them in Markham. I remember being amazed at just how many other people around my age lived within a few blocks. We played outside every night. Soccer, ball hockey, baseball—but most of all, basketball. We'd play on the asphalt at the nearby school for hours, long after the sun went down.

The common ground in my relationship with my mother was always sports. We connected through our mutual interest—or maybe, she made sure to connect with me through sports because she knew it was my passion.

She ran track in high school in Trinidad, where she grew up and lived before moving to Canada when she was 26. I used to hear stories from her siblings about how fast she was back then. Her speciality, of course, was running the 100 and 200 metres. But I never saw it for myself. She didn't mind though. Mom just wanted me to play the sports I loved. She found joy in the excitement I got out of playing.

When we were together at home, we always watched sports. We'd watch Toronto Raptors games in the winter, while I dreamed of being an NBA star. That was when she had the Raptors logo painted on my wall. In the summer it was baseball. I watched the Blue Jays a lot—back in the days of Roy Halladay. I've always been a fan, later riding the excitement of the Edwin Encarnacion and Jose Bautista years. We also watched soccer all the time. I used to be able to tell her the names of all the European players each weekend. She was amazed that, for all of my energy, I could just sit with her and watch a soccer game, completely captivated.

The first sport I actually excelled at was soccer, which I started playing competitively while we still lived in Scarborough. After the move, I kept playing for the Scarborough Azzurri team.

Through the summers when I was in high school, I played rep softball for Scarborough East, which was one of the best teams around. I played shortstop and centre field. I even hit a few home runs as well. Despite the added distance, Mom let me stay with the team after we moved to Markham, which meant I had to make it out to every game and practice even though I lived farther away than the other players. One year, when I was in high school, we beat Kitchener in the provincial finals. That was probably the first incredible experience I had in sports—the kind of exhilaration that comes with winning, celebrating with your teammates, and sharing that joy with the people you love.

As I said before, basketball was really my passion. That's the sport I played competitively every fall and winter. It was where I excelled the most. And my mother always encouraged me to pursue that dream. I played on the junior basketball team in Grade 9. And then in Grade 10, my school wanted me to play on the senior team. I was a good player, and I started to focus on basketball more than any other sport because I knew I needed to if I was going to have any sort of future as an athlete. At least that's what I thought at the time. My mom would send me to skill development camps, finding the money required to make sure I had the best opportunities to improve. And despite working all the time, Mom always made sure she was able to take me to my practices and games. She would sit and watch every minute, whether it was an actual game or just a practice. She took me everywhere. She would take me to my basketball games; she would take me to my soccer games. I'd have tournaments in Buffalo, Niagara Falls, and all over Ontario. She would drop work and go on the road with me. We drove all over the place together.

It's hard to explain the bond we have. We were just always together. Everything I did, she was always there. Almost every memory I have involves her. Every moment.

I didn't know the significance of that bond when I was young. It was just always the two of us. It was who we were.

Mom shielded me from all the stuff she was going through in her life and all the sacrifices she made to give me everything I could need. I didn't realize just how much my mother had done for me until I was getting ready to leave for college. There was a very practical reason for that revelation. All of a sudden, I realized I was going to need some money! When you're growing up you don't have a concept of how much all the activities you do cost—let alone how much it costs to feed and clothe you. But when you're heading out on your own for the first time, that cost becomes apparent very quickly.

I started to appreciate the true cost of her love for me when I left home. As I mentioned, I only had a partial scholarship to the junior college in Coffeyville, so we still had to pay for a lot of stuff.

The scholarship covered tuition, but we had to cover boarding, food, and other living expenses like that. Mom scrambled up some more money and gave me everything she could to make that happen. She'd send me money just to make sure I was taken care of.

Being away from home in Coffeyville was the first time I had to figure things out for myself. My mother had taught me stuff, but I had a lot to learn. She always did everything for me. She *wanted* to do everything for me. I was her little boy. But as I grew up and went out on my own, I had to learn how to fend for myself.

I guess that's where a father comes in. Someone who will teach you about the other stuff to do: a "man's job," so to speak.

I knew my father, but we weren't very close through the first decade of my life because he and my mom had their differences and went separate ways. I was his third child of four. His first two kids are several years older than me—Alexandra and Julian—and I wouldn't meet them until I was about 10 years old. I also have a younger sister, Dantee.

I do have many fond memories of my father, who was a vibrant and widely adored man. But we didn't have the same kind of connection that I had with my mother, who raised me and whom I saw every day. Although I wish our relationship could have been closer, I don't blame him for that. It's something I will get into a bit later.

When I was offered a full scholarship at the University of Southern California in 2014, after two years at Coffeyville, it was the first time my mother didn't need to worry about putting together enough money to make sure I was okay. Everything was covered now. That alone felt like an impossible dream. Of course, Mom still sent whatever extra money she could, to make sure I could pay for anything I needed or wanted to do outside of school.

It's amazing how quickly your perspective changes when you reach adulthood and can finally see what a parent's love looks like. As a kid you never fully understand the sacrifices they make for you. You realize afterwards—wow, you took me to all these places, you worked all those hours, you guided me through all these things.

At the heart of everything, my mother is the kind of athlete, person, and parent I strive to be every day.

I've since moved my mom to a larger house in Pickering, a little farther east. It was one of the biggest joys I've experienced in my career: to give her a home, like she gave me.

Whenever I'm back in Toronto, I still stay with her. It's a constant comfort amid the busy and stressful reality of being a pro athlete. Each visit is a reminder of why I have the privilege of doing what I do—and why I can continue to strive to be the best person and athlete I can be. It's a reminder of how lucky I am to have been raised by a woman like her, a reminder of what truly matters.

My mother remains a constant source of guidance for me. Because of her, I understand the value of sacrifice. I've witnessed the strength that comes with humility. The grace of generosity. And the importance of being patient but firm. Through my mother I have a living example of what success looks like. She's the very best of who I am and who I want to be.

8

NO DOUBT

At the start of my career, I faced a lot of doubters. Many people thought I should focus on the 200 metres and leave the 100-metre race alone.

"You don't have a good enough start," I remember people saying. "The 200 is more your race. You should just do that."

When I first started running, I let that doubt get to me at times. I was a relative amateur compared with many of my competitors. Even though I'd come a long way, I wasn't sure what my limitations were. I sometimes let that get to me.

But doubting what you are capable of before you even try is accepting defeat. That was something I was never able to do. Despite the doubt I felt at times, the more that people tried to convince me of my limitations the more determined I became to prove them wrong. Many of us face that kind of internal struggle, where our doubt and ambition clash.

One of the questions I've learned to ask myself in times of doubt is very simple: *Why not me?*

When people try to put a limit on you and what you can achieve, I think it's wise to ask yourself why they are doing that and whether you agree. The only opinion that matters when it comes to achieving peak performance is yours. What do you believe you are capable of?

Make that your goal and set out to reach it.

When I first realized I might have a chance to build a career as a track athlete, I knew the kind of career I wanted to have. When you think of the greatest track athletes in history, most competed in multiple events. Usain Bolt and Carl Lewis both ran the 100 metres and 200 metres. Michael Johnson ran the 200 and 400.

From the start, those were the names I strived to be compared to. I always felt like that's what makes people great in the sport: when they can excel at more than one thing. That's what I wanted to do. I wanted to be known for my ability to do both at a high level.

That journey started for me when I made the move to the University of Southern California, when I was 19 years old. Of course, it wasn't always a journey filled with confidence. It took the support of people who believed in me to really see that potential in myself.

By the time I made the leap to the NCAA in 2014, I'd caught up to other sprinters my age in terms of ability and skill. That meant I'd made up a lot of ground. But I knew I was still in the early stages of what I was capable of.

I'd been recruited by several top-level schools at the time, but

USC stood out. It wasn't just about the campus in Los Angeles or the prestigious reputation of the school—though that helped. Really it was about the people. Quincy Watts, a former Olympian who was an assistant coach at USC, flew up to Toronto to meet me and my mom in the middle of a winter snowstorm. Then head coach Caryl Smith Gilbert decided she wanted to experience some Canadian weather too. She visited us when a storm knocked out power on my block. I connected with Coach Quincy and Coach Caryl right away. I was confident they could take me to the next level.

That year I made the choice to specialize in both the 100 metres and 200 metres, at the insistence of Coach Caryl. She has a wonderful personality. Her kind spirit is contagious. She was an incredible, inspiring coach—the kind who makes it easy to believe in yourself, because she shows that you can accomplish difficult things. She was the kind of person you just wanted to please all the time. Caryl is the reason I've pushed myself to compete in both.

I remember being apprehensive at first, testing it out at early NCAA meets that year with USC. The naysayers got into my head. I wasn't getting my best results in either event.

But Coach Caryl was adamant. She warned me to not let people tell me I could only do one thing. She told me I still had a long way to go, but that eventually with enough work, I could master both races.

"No. You can fix this," she said. "You've only been in the sport for so long. I believe you can do both."

Caryl gave me the confidence I needed. She told me that since 1997, when she started coaching college-level athletes, she had never seen someone emerge from junior college to a top-level NCAA program so quickly and with such potential. I can't pretend that didn't give me a boost. I think Caryl also might have been trying to get some extra points for the school to earn the NCAA title, but of course if I could be of any help in achieving that goal, I didn't mind at all.

That winter I worked alongside Caryl and Quincy Watts, who was an assistant coach at the time but is now the head coach at USC. Quincy was a huge inspiration for me. He won gold in the 400 metres and the 4 x 400-metre relay at the Barcelona Olympics in 1992. Quincy told me I was a versatile sprinter. I had the speed and endurance at my age to compete in both events. One day, he said, I'd probably have to choose, but not yet. The trick was in trying to put it all together and make something special happen.

In the spring of 2015, I shocked myself—and the NCAA. I won the Pac-12 100-metre championship in May, running it in 9.97 seconds. It was the first time in my life that I'd run the 100 in under 10 seconds. Then I broke the Canadian record in the 200, running it in 20.03.

It turned out that was just the beginning.

When I arrived at the nationals at the University of Oregon that June, I was still considered an underdog compared with my competitors who'd been recruited and watched for years. People were paying attention, but I think they were still trying to figure out who this 20-year-old from Canada was.

And beyond the world of track, no one knew who I was. I had about 600 followers on Instagram at the time, and the announcers at meets would pronounce my name De Grass-ey (like the hit Canadian television show *Degrassi High*).

Trayvon Bromell, who was at Baylor University at the time,

was the favourite to win the national title at both the 100- and 200-metre distance.

The night before the finals at the national championship, Caryl and Quincy sat me down to show me some video and walk me through the strategy for the next day. I was having issues with my acceleration out of my block starts in the 100 metres. They showed me videos of several of my competitors and tried to convince me I had what it took to beat them. Caryl told me that none of the others could run with me on the top end, which means the final 40 metres.

"All you need to do is start with them," she said.

They must have been able to see I was a little bit unsure. I wanted to be confident, but it was clear I didn't completely believe in myself. What they told me that night has always stuck with me:

"Believe that you belong."

"Nobody can run with you."

"Think big!"

"Andre, why not you?"

That question connected. That night, I asked myself a very simple question: *NCAA champion? World champion? Olympic champion? Why not me?*

I'd already come so far in such a short period of time. Sometimes it was almost overwhelming. Everything I had set out to accomplish so far, I had. Even when I doubted myself, I'd found a way to reach the next level.

When I lined up for the 100-metre final the next day, those words lingered in my head: *Why not me?*

When the gun went off, I stayed in line with the other sprinters through the first 10 metres. Caryl says she knew right then that I won the 100.

"Race over," she said, standing on the sidelines a few seconds after the gun. Another coach looked at her like she was nuts.

But Caryl was right. I just kept accelerating, leaving the others several strides behind. I crossed the line in 9.75 seconds to win the national championship.

"Andre De Grass-ey is going to win this," the announcer said, his voice rising. "De Grass-ey beating Bromell! An upset!"

The crowd seemed confused by the win. But Caryl knew—and because of her, I knew too. I didn't *just belong*. I was the national champ! I was astonished and proud. Forget everyone else; I'd proven something to myself.

But there wasn't much time to celebrate. There was even more to prove. As we walked towards the starting blocks in the 200-metre final less than an hour later, Caryl predicted that I was about to do something I had never done before.

"This is your best event. They don't even know you yet. You're about to do your best work," she said. "You're about to do something that's never been done. You're going to run 19.70."

That seemed absurd.

"I am?"

"Yep," she said.

I'd never run that fast in my life. I just smiled at her and shook my head. But it was a boost of confidence that I needed.

The doubters were paying attention now. The ESPN broadcast of the national championship made a big deal out of my 100-metre win and what it meant. I'd beaten the favourite in Trayvon, which set up a showdown storyline between us in the 200.

"I think the whole complexion of this race changes now that Andre De Grass-ey ran 9.75 with a 2.7 wind," the commentator said.

"Who knows what he might do now with that 100-metre under his belt. Bromell is looking for redemption. It should be a barn burner."

It wasn't.

I took off out of the blocks, just the way Caryl and I planned. I accelerated through the turn and knew it was mine. The other guys just couldn't stay with me.

I crossed the line in 19.58 seconds to win the national championship, a super-fast time that would have been an official NCAA record had I not benefited from an illegal tailwind.

I was shocked. Caryl was shocked. She believed I could win but had no idea I'd pull off a performance like that.

"His improvement is staggering," the broadcaster said. "Just staggering."

Up to that moment, I had never felt the joy of victory like that. I'd just become the NCAA champion in both the 100 and 200 metres, setting an all-conditions record in the 200-metre (meaning I'd posted the fastest time ever, but the wind at my back meant the result wasn't an official record). From that moment on, I knew I wanted to dominate both events.

So much changed overnight for me after the national championship. My story made national news back home in Canada. My phone battery kept dying because there were so many notifications coming through with messages from people congratulating me. By the next day, I had almost 10,000 Instagram followers.

Looking back now, I understand that being crowned the NCAA's 100- and 200-metre champion was the beginning of something special. It was the moment everything changed.

That's been my goal ever since. I want to be known as "a guy who can run both"—like the all-time greats. Canada's Percy

Williams won gold in the 100 and 200 at the 1928 Olympics in Amsterdam. In 1936, the legendary Jesse Owens won gold in both events representing the United States—and added two more in the long jump and 4 x 100-metre relay—in a historic performance at the Berlin Olympics, a defiant triumph in the shadow of Nazi Germany. Only two other athletes, American Bobby Morrow in 1956 and Valeriy Borzov, representing the Soviet Union in 1972, won gold in both events before Carl Lewis dazzled the world with his untouchable performances at the 1984 and 1988 Olympics. And then there was Bolt, who won gold in both events in three straight Olympic Games—2008, 2012, and 2016.

In my world, Bolt and Lewis set the bar. The fact that so few have done it before makes it all the more appealing. Before I retire, I hope to add my name to the list of athletes who have won Olympic gold in both events.

I've gotten to a point where I've consistently medalled in both throughout my career. I've shown that I can do it. But winning gold in both events on the biggest stage is a tough target, and there are limited chances to hit it.

I've never regretted the decision to specialize in both the 100 and 200 metres. Even though it's a tough challenge, I know I'm much more satisfied having set out to succeed in both, instead of limiting myself to a single event.

Today, it's still a complicating aspect in my career. It seems like every year the conversation over whether I should continue to run both events comes up. I've been criticized for trying to take on too much. If I would just focus on running the 100 or the 200, I would have more time to rest and recover. My training could also be much more focused and possibly more effective. That's one perspective. But I don't think it considers the whole picture.

There's the pride factor, of course. I want to be considered among the all-time greats. But it's also about using the opportunity I have with the gifts I have, while I am able to. The truth is, competing in both races is more lucrative than limiting myself to one. Double the events is double the exposure. And running both the 100 and 200 metres doesn't just appeal to the pride of athletes—it's a narrative that appeals to fans.

Sprinting isn't just a passion for me. This is my career. It's how I support my family, and it's an opportunity to give them everything they need in life. I've made the decision to take a more challenging approach to my career because it's about carving out my legacy and my financial future. Both are true. Both motivate me.

Training for both events is hard because the races require such different game plans. The 100 metres is about being explosive and aggressive. It's about getting out of those blocks as quickly as possible, maintaining your form, and breathing. You power towards your top speed—between the 30- and 60-metre range—and then hold your top end for the last 30 to 40 metres. The 200 is much more strategic. You want to start strong but then as you reach 80 to 110 metres, as you're whipping around the corner, you find a second burst—almost like you're zipping downhill on skis, gaining momentum. Once you get to that top speed you want to hold your form through the final 60 metres. Even though it's still a sprint, it requires a special kind of endurance. Training requires a balance. It's different with each coach, but generally we end up working three days a week on the 100 and two days on the 200, with a third day focused on a mixture of approaches to training for both.

I still love it, but I also know I can't do this forever. Eventually I'm going to realize I just don't have it in me anymore. Later in my career, as I start to get older and wear down, I might have to choose one event and stick with it. Every year the training gets a little bit harder than it was the year before. That's normal. That's life. But it's especially true when you're training for two events. You get a sense of what your body is capable of. Part of you just knows. While I've faced several injuries in my career, I've actually been pretty fortunate to have held up as well as I have.

Beyond the injuries, the overall physical strain is even more taxing; your body starts to break down in ways you never imagined it could. But it also becomes a challenge from a mental standpoint as you balance internal and external expectations—on top of the everyday struggles of life.

But that day hasn't come yet. I hope it's still far away. I've been lucky so far. I've been fortunate that my body has held up, despite some frustrations along the way. I'm grateful for that. And I'm still young. I *feel* like I'm still young anyway. The reality is that an athlete nearing 30 is usually nearing the back end of their career. The transition from young to old as an athlete happens so quickly.

With that reality in mind, I've promised myself that I will try to compete in both events for as long as I am able. I'm still laser focused on winning double gold at the Olympics. I came close in Tokyo, but not close enough.

I'm not satisfied yet. I can't be.

But even now as an Olympic gold medallist, I still find that I need to revisit the lesson I first learned in college. Self-doubt is normal. It helps drive us to be better. But it can also defeat us if we let it.

Whenever I doubt myself, even today, I revisit that lesson I first learned in college. I think it's a lesson that anyone facing a task that feels insurmountable can learn from. One of the biggest obstacles to our ability to perform is our own perception of our limitations. Don't let it be.

Instead, ask yourself that simple question—and consider the answer: *Why not me?*

9

YOU VS. YOU

I've been told many times that my most effective tool as a competitor is my ability to relax—to be *chill*—at the right moment.

For a lot of people, that's hard. It's difficult for me too. People often say I don't seem nervous before a race, but that's not really true. It's impossible to not feel the pressure. The stakes, sometimes, are enormous. In track, you have a small window to perform exceptionally well. The World Athletics Championships takes place every two years. The Olympics are held every four years. There are only three podium spots.

To succeed the way you've dreamed of—the way you've worked so hard to—everything has got to be almost perfect. Everything has to be clicking at exactly the right time.

That's definitely added pressure. You need to have a lot of focus. You need to be mentally strong. Not just physically strong but mentally as well. I believe that once you've reached a certain level, peak performance in track is 90 percent mental and 10 percent physical.

That pressure can be good or bad, depending on how you address it.

Many high-performance athletes work with a sport psychologist or mental performance coach to help them focus and deal with pressure. But I've never actually worked with one. When I suffered a serious hamstring injury that threatened my career, a lot of people recommended that I speak with a sport psychologist to guide me through the process. It was a difficult time, probably the lowest point of my life. But even then, it wasn't something I pursued.

It's not that I have anything against working with a specialist like that. There's a lot of value in it. As athletes we need whatever edge we can get. If it helps, it's worth it.

I've been fortunate to have good people around me to talk to about what's going on in my life. That has always helped. Having a support system is so important. Far too often, many people feel like they are on their own, with nobody in their corner cheering them on, loving them, and guiding them. I'm blessed by the people around me who lift me up every day. Knowing that not everyone has the same kind of support in their life, or may not be comfortable opening up to people around them, is part of the reason I became an ambassador for Kids Help Phone. Now, maybe more than ever, young people need to feel that support in their lives. They need to know there are people who believe in them and are there to help.

///////

My old coach Tony and the friends I grew up with always tell me the same thing: it's crazy how I came into the sport of track and field. This wasn't something I started as a young kid. It just happened out of the blue. So I take it in stride. I always remember to just have fun with it. I try not to take it too seriously or get overwhelmed by the gravity of it all. I know some people in sports are always studying their craft. And I do that as well, but not obsessively.

In moments where it does feel overwhelming, I shift my mind away from track. I don't like to think about it too much. That might sound counterintuitive, but I don't believe it is. Pressure mounts when you become too singularly focused on one thing or the success you so desperately want to realize, without keeping the situation in perspective. If I have confidence in my preparation, getting wound up about the race itself isn't going to do anything but hurt me. This is what it means to trust in the process. You have faith in the work you put in to get to that moment. You've already determined your best outcome in the months, weeks, and days that got you there.

So sometimes it's okay to just take a break, reset, and come back to it. I'll watch a funny show, play video games, or spend time with my kids—anything to take my mind off the pressure. To just *get away*. After a pause like that, it's time to reset and return to track, giving it my full attention and effort. I don't know if other sprinters do this or not, but it's what helps me cope with the pressure of having success or defeat riding on a performance that lasts for mere seconds.

In the first round of any big event, I'm always trying to get the jitters out. I'm a little bit nervous when I step into that stadium. I almost always have to remind myself to take a deep breath. I need to soak in the moment. I need to recognize what it took to get to where I am. This is one more chance to show the world that I belong. Once I take a few beats to process the moment, I know I'm ready to go.

Right before each race, as I am about to step into the blocks, I follow the same routine: I take a long, deep breath and focus on my cues. I don't think about who is standing beside me, or who is watching in the stands, or how many are watching at home. I don't think about what is at stake in that particular race. I zero in on the task and block out all the noise. Once I'm in that zone—my heart beating fast but my mind locked in—I listen for the gun. The adrenalin kicks in.

Crack.

That's the only sound that matters in that moment. Once I hear the gun, I react as fast as I can to push off the blocks. The speed of that reaction is usually the difference between landing a spot on the podium and failing to reach it.

That reaction needs to be exact. If you lose your focus and jump the gun, it's over. When a sprinter is too wound up, they get in their own head. They try to anticipate the gun instead of reacting to it.

To have success, you need to drown out the distractions, both internal and external. You have to block out the noise.

Many people struggle with that, at least a little bit. It takes a lot of practice.

I struggled with it early on in my career. I messed up all the time when I was training under Tony Sharpe in those first few months of my life as a sprinter. My reaction times were all over the place.

Tony would get me to line up on the blocks and then he'd shout "set" and I'd rise into position, my legs loaded into the blocks and ready to fire. But I'd always start a second too early or a second too late—I never seemed to be able to start the instant I heard that whistle blast.

"Come on, man, react to the whistle!" Tony would shout. "You have to react!"

I'd get so flustered. I just couldn't get the timing down. I'd get nervous and take off too soon, or I'd try too hard to be patient and end up starting way too late. It was frustrating because there isn't a way to be taught how to react. There isn't an instant fix to make your nervous system respond more quickly aside from practice and doing drills that develop that speed. That was all I could do—start after start, again and again.

It wasn't going to happen overnight. Few things do. You need to get enough reps in until the reaction becomes a habit, something so natural you don't consciously think about it. You need to find the rhythm to a start.

Eventually, it began to come naturally, but it took me a while to get the timing right. I had to find a balance between my intensity and calmness. It's still a struggle. Before races I'll do drills to get my nervous system firing so that when it's time to perform, I'm alert and ready for action.

The reality is that everyone gets nervous on the line, just like many people get nervous when they face a stressful moment in their lives in which they have to perform. The trick is figuring out a way to calm those nerves. In a tense moment, you need to pause and remind yourself to settle in. Otherwise, your nerves will take over.

I've seen competitors on the blocks get so caught up in the

tension of the moment that they false-start perpetually. A couple of disqualifications in a row will do that to you. Instead of thinking about the finish line, they are caught at the start. It's a psychological thing, for sure.

It's tough, whether you're standing in front of 80,000 in a stadium in Beijing or a hundred people at a small high school track meet. The scale doesn't matter because the nervous system is reacting the same way. You've probably felt something like it before, when your entire body starts to tingle and you can feel your heart thumping through your chest. In an environment like that, everything kind of just goes through the roof.

We are all different, so I can't tell you the best way to calm yourself in moments like that. But if you can find a way to recognize and control that moment—by breathing slowly, or maybe zeroing in your focus on the next task—then you can harness those nerves into energy that converts to optimal performance.

There is nothing quite like the hush that falls over a packed stadium the moment an announcer says, "On your marks . . . Shhhh." The entire place, often tens of thousands of people, goes silent.

The quiet is good. The sudden shift from chaos to calm forces you to focus. It locks you in. Now all you're hearing is one collective sound, a still murmur. It's a tense quiet, with everyone waiting for the same sound.

The gun goes off and the roar returns. Everything gets loud. But I can't hear a thing. I'm in the zone from that moment until I cross the finish line. There is nothing but the rumble of spikes hitting the track until the race is over. Then there is a moment, as you're finding your breath, when it's like they turn the volume back on—like a rush of cheers—and everyone is going crazy.

That was one thing I missed in Tokyo when I won the gold medal in the 200 metres in an empty stadium, because of the pandemic. The place was quiet. I carried the excitement, but the roaring soundtrack was on mute. I wish I'd had that crowd factor.

Out of my six races at the Olympics so far, the first three I won silver and bronze in front of a sold-out crowd in Rio, and I heard the noise—but I want to experience that gold moment in front of a crowd as well.

Hopefully I am able to experience that in my career before I'm done. I've experienced it in big stadiums in the Diamond League meets, but nothing beats that feeling at a big event like a World Championships or the Olympics—until I retire, that's what I'm working towards.

Of course, the crowd isn't always cheering for you when you cross the finish line. Often that chorus plays for someone else— and you're left trying to figure out how you managed to fall so far behind.

During a 200-metre race in Doha in 2022, that's what I heard. It was a brutal race. It felt like I heard everyone else running beside me and moving past me. I knew right away I was beat. My legs were dead. On the turn, the guy beside me pulled. That's happened many times before, but it was the way he passed me. He took off while I felt like I was still trying to get off this turn. I knew that race wasn't going to come back to me. There was nothing I could do. I could see two guys well ahead of me already, so I knew I was going to be fighting for third or fourth place. They kept getting farther away, as I found my legs getting heavier and heavier every step.

It was a tough, frustrating race.

This is where the mental component of being a high-performance athlete—and I think high-performance anything—really takes over. It's easy to process a result you are happy with, but it's much more difficult to grapple with defeat. This is why the mental game is so key to achieving peak performance. A bad race, a loss—a poor performance on an assignment, or a terrible day at work—can become much worse if you are not prepared to process and learn from it. I've been haunted by poor performances in the past, obsessing over what went wrong, and it's never benefited me. If anything, it's become a distraction. There was a time in my career where that performance in Doha might have lingered in my mind. But with experience, I've learned to not let it.

That's not to say you can't learn from defeat. It's important to assess what went wrong and to correct what you can. Rather than dwelling on what went wrong, you can review it from the mindset of being constructive. Building off disappointment. I always watch the film of my races and try to determine where things went sideways. Was it a slow start? Was there something off with my mechanics? Were my shoulders too tight? Once I can identify the problem, I determine how to fix it, figure out a next step—and let it go. I bury it in the back of my mind and move on to the next race.

At least that's what I try to do. For the most part, I've been pretty good at leaving the past in the past. It's all mental.

I tell myself: "It's okay. It's just one race."

That might sound cliché, but it doesn't matter, because it's absolutely true. There's a saying in track and field that people don't remember the bad finishes. They only remember the big moments. If you lose one of these races, very few people take note. You just need to try to get it right for the championship.

Because the reality is that you're not going to win every single race. But you always try to—and when you don't, there's always lessons to be learned from those losses.

There are lots of situations in professional life that work like this. You're not always going to bring your best performance. It doesn't matter how obsessed you are with perfection, or how much work you put in to achieve it. If you're human, you're not always going to win. The key is to turn that loss into a future win. Look at the small things in defeat. Find positives where you assume they don't exist.

That terrible race in Doha turned out to be my best time of the season up to that point. I'd been struggling through an injury and a battle with COVID, so a lot of factors were at play. I need to factor those variables into how I view a performance, even though the competitive part of me just wants to be disappointed. It was my best time of the season—and it wasn't even close to my personal best. So you balance it. You look at it both ways, reflecting on the good stuff and some bad stuff, and then sit down with your team and think about what you can do better.

"Don't panic," my coach said after Doha. "It's okay. You didn't have a good start. And you didn't have a top end."

He meant that at the back end of my race, my top speed never arrived. Usually that's my strength. But for some reason, that day, I just didn't have it. When we looked back at my recent races, it was clear that my top-end speed had been declining. A nagging foot injury had kept me from training the way I usually do before the competition season. And even though it didn't feel serious, it was still having a big impact on me.

"You missed a lot of training with your injury, so don't think of it as you're done," he said. "Your time is slowly going down, but once your foot gets back to 100 percent, you'll be back running fast times."

My recent bout with COVID likely also had an effect in ways that were hard for me to realize. Sprinting is a precise sport. In other sports, athletes might be able to compensate for a nagging injury. But when you're standing on the line with only 100 metres to the finish, every single variable plays a role.

My coach assured me that the decline in my top speed was temporary, because of the injury, and there was no other indication I was slowing down. By stepping back, looking at the data, and assessing the circumstances, I was able to walk away from that defeat confident it was just another step in the process of getting back to my peak ability.

I've seen a lot of runners psych themselves out because of a bad result or a rough swing of bad results. But if you're really being competitive, that's something you can't let yourself do. Once you do that, it's over. You defeated yourself. You psyched yourself out. It's hard to come back from that.

I think with track, even though you are racing other people, most of the time you are actually racing against yourself.

If you think about it, this is true when it comes to most challenges in life.

The key is to always remember that regardless of what you are competing in, *you* are your toughest competitor. The situation doesn't matter. Whether I am racing on the Diamond League circuit in Doha or in the Tokyo Olympics, the opponent who matters most is always me. Every other factor is an obstacle I need to overcome in order to be the best version of myself in my performance that day. It's as simple as that.

The difference between achieving my personal best might be a fraction of a millisecond. A race can be decided by the distance between the front of my chest and my back.

You just need to figure out how you can get faster. If you ran this time today, how can you run faster tomorrow?

In most challenges we face, that is the main obstacle.

When you look at it as a matter of how to beat your best time—as opposed to trying to beat someone else—you're moving in the right direction. And when you realize it's *you* versus *you*—and that you're beating your old self every single day, that's when you can accomplish some big things. You're not worried about the rest of the field.

My primary focus in every race I run is *me*. The primary focus in your race should be *you*.

Respect what the others are doing, but try to focus on what you can control. I know my opponents are studying me as much as or more than I am studying them. So as much effort as I put into analyzing them, I put much more into building on my strengths and improving on my weakest areas.

If you do that, it doesn't matter what everyone else does. In the end, it's you versus the clock.

Worry about executing *your* race, whatever that race might be.

10

PREPARE TO SUCCEED

O ne of the many reasons sprinting is unique is that you are competing, for the most part, against the same people repeatedly. There are recurring clashes in other sports, but it's not always on the same scale or frequency with which the top sprinters in the world face each other. LeBron James and Kevin Durant play each other only a few times in a season. Tennis greats like Rafael Nadal and Roger Federer would meet in the late rounds or finals of major tournaments. Christine Sinclair and Abby Wambach starred for Canada and the United States in memorable battles on the pitch between the two nations. But when it comes to every race I run in, there is always someone I have raced against before. And they are always among the fastest people alive.

On the outside, the sport might come across as being very intimate. It's a test of pure athleticism, between the only people who can reach those speeds and potentially beat each other. It's only the best of the best, against one another, in a test of absolute speed and power.

When you have that kind of talent facing off, it seems like it would create a clash of personalities and egos. For a long time, sprinting carried that reputation—looking back to the days of guys like Ben Johnson and Carl Lewis, Donovan Bailey and Michael Johnson. There were some well-known conflicts back then. But the '80s and '90s were a different time. Our generation doesn't play the same game. We'll talk a little bit of crap. But no one really hears it. It doesn't make headlines. You might see a bit of posturing on social media, but it's not in your face, making headlines the way it used to be.

I'm not sure why that is, but it's just not the vibe of our generation of runners. I mean, it's a non-contact sport! And we all know that on any given day, another person has the ability to win. It's funny because I've been told that I come off somewhat humble when it comes to track. But when I play basketball, I don't stop smack-talking. I'm vocal as hell. I'm going to beat you and I'm going to tell you exactly how I'm going to beat you. I think it's hard to do that in track, unless you're showboating—going over the top with poses for the camera and puffing yourself up. That's kind of the only bravado you can effectively show in track. Trash talk is kind of hard—I mean, there are only so many ways you can tell someone you're going to run faster than they are.

I don't have any desire to do that. In fact, I'm genuinely happy for my competitors when they do well. I don't see their success as a threat to my own. The better we all run, the better it is for our sport.

A guy like Aaron Brown, whom I've been running with for years, is often someone I'm racing against—but he's also a close teammate and friend. I've trained alongside Aaron at relay camps for years. I've witnessed the work he puts in. We always joke around about who's going to win the Canadian national title. But we're cool—we're friends.

I look at it this way: when other Canadians are running well, it's good for the program. During the 2022 season, Aaron won his first 100-metre Diamond League race in Birmingham. I fell way behind, dealing with a nagging foot injury, and didn't stand a chance the way he was moving. I was genuinely happy to see him celebrate the win. It was a big moment for him. I think when you've seen someone struggle—you've seen some of the ups and downs—and they have a breakthrough, you've got to feel good about it. That's what it's all about.

It was also a promising moment for Canada. A few months later, Aaron and I would be representing Canada in the 4 x 100-metre relay at the Oregon World Championships. Seeing how well Aaron was running at the time, I knew we were going to do something special—and I was right.

I'm a fan of my competitors, and I've learned a lot from watching them and racing beside them. But I've also learned the importance of understanding the strengths and weaknesses of my opponents, and using those insights to build a better strategy to defeat them. This is a lesson that can be applied to any level of competition, in sport or in the workplace. Know who is racing to beat you, and prepare your game plan with that in mind. In any competition, it's valuable to understand your opponents' strengths and weaknesses—and how they view yours.

Over the years this has become a more critical element in how I prepare for races. So much of it is done behind the scenes.

I'll watch other runners compete to see how they approach their races—how they use their strengths and compensate for their weaknesses. I want to know what to expect in a race, so I'm not taken by surprise and panic.

For example, I know that Christian Coleman and Trayvon Bromell have a strong start. They both explode out of the blocks. I study their strengths, so I know where I need to improve to counter them. When I'm standing on the line with guys like Coleman and Bromell, I know if I can just stick with them through the first 20 metres of a race then I'll put myself in a position to win.

But beforehand, as I prepare with my coach, we'll break down the strengths and weaknesses of the other runners. We'll get the most up-to-date information on my opponents' recent races and see what their times look like at different parts of the race. My coach will tell me how quickly they run 30 metres and lay out a plan to attack my race with that in mind. If we can get my timing down in practice, working on starts to 30 metres, then I'm going to stick with them. We know I have better top-end speed, so if I can catch them in those first 30 metres, the race is over. I'm going to win.

That's how we look at it. If I can take care of my business at the right time, my strengths will beat theirs.

My girlfriend, Nia Ali—a world champion and an Olympic medallist in the 100-metre hurdles—uses knowledge of other runners to much more strategic advantage than I do. As a hurdler, she focuses a lot more on what other athletes are doing. She has a better sense of her opponents' approach to their races than I do with mine. Hurdles are much more technical than sprints, so Nia is more strategic about it than I am. There is a lot more happening from the start to the finish over those 100 metres. Nia watches her opponents and knows which are good starters and which are better on the back end. She knows how they approach their races. There are moments in the race where she can put pressure on another runner and get in their head, gaining a critical edge.

I'm not nearly as focused on that aspect in my preparation as Nia is. We just have different approaches, which both work for us. When I'm on the line, I don't think about it—all that stuff kind of falls apart and I end up just racing.

That's why preparation is critical. There really isn't time to think about strategy in the moments before the gun goes off. This is the moment of focus, where you just need to believe you've studied the game plan well enough in practice that it becomes automatic when it matters. If you're distracted, you're unlikely to stick to the strategy. This is where you have got to focus and make sure you don't fall apart.

It happens to all of us at some point. The race begins and you get startled by a slow reaction on the start and you're trying to play catch-up too quickly—and you burn out. All of your timing is messed up and the entire game plan is tossed out. It happens so fast. It's like a chain reaction in which every action leads to the next, but none of it works as you planned. And now the person beside you passes by and you have no gas left to catch them.

Strategy also is key when you're running in heats trying to reach the final. You need to have a game plan throughout the rounds so you're rolling by the time you reach the final. You need to qualify, but you don't want to burn out in the first round or the semis. If you're tired after two rounds, you're beat. You want to make sure you can lay out a max effort in that final.

The strategy also changes depending on what lane you are in.

Many people don't know how much a lane draw can affect runners in an event like the 200.

Your game plan changes depending on where you stand on the curve in the event's staggered start. If you're in lane seven, there's only one person in front of you. So you need to catch them—and once you catch them, you've got to go. You've got to take that lead right away and make sure you stay relaxed and stay calm—because when somebody comes up on you, you don't want to panic.

But if you start in the middle of the track, you have a better perspective on everything right away. You know how to judge what's kind of going on around you. Off the gun, you can see the guys on the outside lane and hear the guys on the inside lane. You can judge where you are within the mix. I can relax while I'm running, knowing I'm in a good position and can hold that speed until I get off the turn and put on the jets. Everything kind of falls into place if you time it right, so that you're hitting your top speed as others have nothing left to give. It's all about timing. You can't wait too long, and you can't make it happen too early. There is a sweet spot, found through hours of practice.

This all might sound crazy to someone who isn't a sprinter, because it's only 10 or 20 seconds. But this process automatically goes through your mind when you have planned ahead, understand your opponents, and have a game plan. All of this gets broken down in your head as your legs are firing and you're flying down the track. You want to be in a zone where this process flows—rather than worrying about catching up or whether you've got enough left in you to hold off an opponent at the line.

When you reach the final, you don't want to be thinking about any of this. By that time, you're not focused on everybody else.

If you've been successful, you've managed to conserve enough energy as possible through your heat and the semis. Now you've just got to trust that you'll execute your plan and hope it works.

Usually, you know what lane you're in the night before. You also know who will be lined up next to you, so you know what to expect from them. I think about all the phases of my race and what I need to do to put myself in a position to win. If you know the runner on your left is a good starter, you anticipate that they are coming up on you right off the start, so you remind yourself to not panic when that happens. If they are a slow starter you've got to use that to your advantage. You've got to build a lead on them right away and hold it, because they are going to be a good finisher. You can't let their top speed reach yours. You've got to hold that lead past 50 metres and keep hitting your stride, because you know they are coming.

Regardless of what you are setting out to achieve, the opponents trying to get there too are just obstacles in that pursuit. Putting in the effort to study them, to understand how they operate, and to learn from them is only going to equip you with better information to build a better game plan in competition.

Any goal we set out to achieve requires proper preparation to get there. Life isn't full of the kind of direct competition I face as a sprinter, with the aim of being the fastest on the track. But regardless of what our specific goals are, we have put in the time and effort to ensure that we are our best when it comes time to perform. As one of my favourite sayings goes, "Failing to prepare is preparing to fail."

11

FIND YOUR ZONE

For me, a race itself is only a fraction of a minute. But it really begins the day before that flash in time. I think every athlete is different, but I get into a focused mindset two to three hours before the race. Sometimes even longer.

I don't even remember what I felt the night before the 200-metre final at the Tokyo Olympics, but I know I was already getting into a zone. You almost forget what goes through your mind in those moments because you're so wired.

I begin entering my zone when I start making sure I've got everything ready to race. I start lacing up my shoes. I make sure my kit is together. I put on my headphones and start listening to music to hype me up. The genre depends on the day. It can be hip hop, it can be rap, it can be reggae. Sometimes it's R&B. It's a matter of my vibe at the moment. I just have a feel for what I need at the time. There will always be a song I pick that is going to give me this mental push. It's not always about beats. Sometimes it's about lyrics for me too. I enjoy artists who have a message. And on race day, there is always a message I need to hear. I want to feel something. Music is so inspirational in that way. Everyone's wired differently. We all connect to different things. But I don't know a person who doesn't love music.

I have a lot of inner dialogue with myself. I tend to get lost in my head sometimes, especially before a race—but sometimes just in everyday life.

When I seem zoned out, my girlfriend Nia always asks me if I'm talking to myself. I usually am. It's like I'm locked into a thought and I can't get out of it. Often she'll hear me talking when I'm in the shower.

"Are you talking to yourself?" she'll ask with a laugh.

Yep, I absolutely am.

"No. What are you talking about?" I'll shout back. "I think you're hearing stuff."

And then I'm stuck thinking, "Well, I was thinking about something—but now I'm not because you're over there ruining my thoughts!"

Sometimes, especially before a race, I don't even realize I'm actually talking to myself out loud. I'll be in my zone, listening to my music—and someone will look at me kind of funny and ask if I'm okay. It's like they think there is something wrong with me.

I don't mind though. Well, maybe when Nia gives me a hard time for zoning out at home. But not when I'm about to race. That's when my head needs to be in a place only I can understand.

If you've ever faced a high-pressure situation where you need to focus and perform, you probably know what I'm talking about.

You just kind of do it. I don't think there is a set process for getting in the zone that I can pass on to anyone. We are all differ-ent—as is the process our brains use to get us ready to perform. I think the most important thing is to find a way that works for you.

Right before a race, I need to be on my own. It's a quiet zone. I don't want to be disturbed.

It's kind of like a pitcher in baseball who doesn't speak to the press on the day they are pitching—or a goalie in hockey who is a complete recluse on game day. You don't speak to them; they don't speak to you. Everyone is happy—because everyone knows you need to get into a zone to perform, especially in a high-stress position that requires a lot of focus.

Sometimes people will try to speak to me, and it's probably one of the few times where you'll see me visibly annoyed. It's often something very well meaning. They'll ask me if I saw what lane I'm in—or whether I'm ready for the race.

"Yeah, man," I think. "Stop talking to me. I have my head-phones on!"

I never say that, of course. I'll just nod an answer and hope the conversation doesn't linger. Usually they get the vibe pretty quickly. If they need to talk to me—for some kind of instruction about the race, or something like that—they'll tell me quickly and move on. But some people don't quite get it, and I'm stuck in a conversation that I really don't want to be having—or don't have time to be having. So I'm nodding politely, but in my head, I'm thinking, "Stop talking to me!"

I *know* there are people out there who can appreciate that. I can't be the only one!

I just want to be on my own, in my quiet zone. Most people around me know that about me, so it is usually not a problem.

They say that when I'm locked in and I'm focused, I need to be left in my world. Shutting out the noise around us every once in a while can be very helpful for anyone looking to get focused and find their zone.

Depending on where I'm racing, it can be tough, because sometimes I'm put in a position where I can't be alone. During a recent race in Italy, that was the case. It was a small meet in a beautiful little town outside of Venice that my agent signed me up for between Diamond League events. It was a nice track, in a gorgeous setting. But the organizers must not have considered the need for security—or even a warm-up area. The spectators were allowed to be everywhere. It was crazy. So as I was trying to warm up, people kept coming up to me asking for autographs and photos. Of course I said yes. I'm always going to be nice to fans. Anytime someone wants to meet you, it's an honour. And Italians are very nice people. I was happy to meet them. But it meant I didn't get any warm-up time. I wasn't able to get into my zone *at all*. It was probably the first time something like that had happened to me at a professional event.

Every time I thought I was going to get a chance to settle into my music and my thoughts, someone new would come up to speak with me or pose for another photo.

The race didn't go well. I almost came last.

Afterwards I told Paul, my track agent, that it was the last time we were doing an off-the-radar meet like that.

"Don't ever take me to a small meet again," I said. I didn't care how much they were willing to pay.

In the end, I'm laughing about it. I mean, it was a trip to a beautiful place in Italy. But as far as performances go, I was terrible. And the only real reason is that I wasn't able to prepare the way I usually do.

Routines work. If you want to perform your best, you need to put yourself in a zone that will allow you to focus and execute. So talk to yourself in the shower, listen to music—hey, even snap photos with strangers, if that's what works. And this doesn't apply just to sports. Whatever your pursuit is, if you want to be your best, find a routine and stick with what works (regardless of how silly it might seem). It might be a test in school or a big presentation in front of your co-workers or a client. It could just be a mindset you need to get in to execute a task well. Focus is such a critical element in achieving peak performance. Our routines put us in the mental space we need to be in to be our best. Make yours a priority that you refuse to waver from.

12

REST, REBUILD, REPEAT

When I arrived at the Tokyo Olympics in July 2021, I felt a ton of pressure. It's hard to describe exactly what spins through my mind in moments like that, with so much on the line. Of course, there was all the personal expectation that I carried. But I could also feel the expectation of everyone hoping I would succeed.

I wanted to do big things. I wanted to make my country proud. I wanted to make my family and my friends proud. None of them could be there with me because of the COVID pandemic, but that only made me more aware that everyone was watching from home. I didn't want to let them down. It's funny how we are always looking for approval. It reminds me of being a kid. My daughter is always calling out to me saying, "Look, Daddy! Look, Daddy!" whenever she does something she hopes will impress me. I kind of look at the outside pressure of performance like that. I want to impress everyone. I don't want to let anyone down.

I'm certain this is a common feeling. You don't need to stand on the line at the Olympics to feel pressure. We all have responsibilities, however common they might seem, that put pressure on us to perform our best. We all understand the fear of not performing our best and of letting the people who believe in us down. It's a human emotion, whether you're an Olympic athlete or not.

That pressure is natural, and if you can learn to harness it, it can be very positive. But we also need to develop the tools to control it. Throughout my career, I've learned the value of looking ahead and knowing when you need to be your best.

Through training and preparation, it's possible to create a road map that allows you to be your best right when you need to be. It requires thinking about the task not just as something in the future, but as something you're setting the course for right now. This can be applied to everything from a student preparing for a final test to a CEO setting a course for the business objectives his company needs to achieve. There are ebbs and flows in that pursuit—and unexpected detours—but in the end, it's always about keeping the key target in mind.

After everything I'd been through to get to Tokyo, I knew I was going to feel some pressure rising. But I'd learned through past experiences that I can control those anxieties through preparation.

When I've put in the work beforehand, it feels like everything is moving in a circle, like a storm building and moving across the land ready to unleash something big. It's all working together, flowing at the right time. That's how I view it. All these factors play a big role in my performance. What matters most is that everything is clicking when it needs to be.

I've always felt confident that if I've put in that extra work, if training is going well, I'm eating right, I'm hydrated—if everything is clicking—then I've put myself in a position to be my best. It gives me confidence to know my coach is happy with how I'm performing and that my physical therapist feels things are going well with my body.

When I was a student at USC, I took a class called stress management. It was one of my favourite classes. It took us through basic steps on how to mitigate anxious situations. One of the key pieces of advice that helped me was to write things down to keep track of my preparation.

Keeping records of key components of performance like nutrition, hydration, and sleep so you can reflect on how you've taken care of your body helps you quantify your own preparation. By keeping track of what you have done to put yourself in a position to succeed, you create a visual way to counter the doubt that creeps into your mind about whether you are ready to perform at your best.

When you're eating right, hydrating right, and sleeping right, your stress levels go down and you don't feel as overwhelmed. When your mind is racing, sometimes all you need is to slow down. I've found that writing things down has been a huge help for me. It allows me to quantify the work and preparation I have put in, which gives me a logical perspective to counter that rising anxiety. It's just a simple habit I've found has a big effect on my mental well-being.

My routine training also incorporates practices that help mitigate stress. At USC we did yoga regularly. I found it helpful to just slow down and breathe. Although I don't formally do yoga today, I've taken simple techniques that I learned through yoga and implemented them in my everyday life. I'll take time out regularly to just sit and breathe for about 10 minutes. I clear my head of all distractions. I don't worry about upcoming races, training, or regular stress that comes with being an adult and a father. I just relax and calm myself.

Depending on where I am at the time, I'll try to take it outside. I find that being in nature helps calm things down even more. A quick walk with the dog works for me. But you can also just be chilling on your couch or lying in bed. Wherever you are, those little techniques help you relax and take your mind off things when stressful situations mount.

These techniques have helped me bounce back from disappointments. If I know I had a bad race, I can settle my anxiety. I tell myself to take it one step at a time. Let's get through today and then let's get through tomorrow. And we'll go from there. I don't try to think too far ahead. I have confidence in my preparation and process.

Success is found in the culmination of that complete, collective effort. It's about learning to have confidence in yourself and in the work you have put in up to the point of execution—and to stick to a plan even when things don't turn out the way you'd hoped. To succeed you have to believe you deserve to be in the position you're in. For me, I know I'm one of the best on the line. It's not a fluke that I'm standing there, just like it's not a fluke when anyone else is in a position to achieve something great. You've earned that opportunity. The challenge now is to prove it to yourself. You have nothing to prove to anyone else.

For me, I know that I am capable of being one of the fastest people in the world. I've been doing it in practice. I've been improving. My coach will tell me my times, encouraging me—letting me know I'm on the verge of breaking a personal best or a world record, or whatever it is.

Your situation might be different. But you've also had success. You need to believe in that success. You have to know you belong—and now you have to put it together when it counts. That's the mental part of the race: knowing you did everything you could.

Then you tell yourself: "It's time to go. It's time to actually prove it now—and not just in practice."

That's why I continue to work hard and not give up on myself and quit. There are days when I want to. Trust me. Even now, training can be rough. I recently finished a big workout session, using a machine called a 1080. We use it to do resistance workouts and overspeed workouts. It can pull you at different speeds or resist you at different weights. It's a pretty basic concept. But it's tough as hell.

The idea is that this kind of training helps you build speed. It helps you get faster by getting you used to the rhythm of moving faster than you normally do. When you reach top speeds with assistance, your body gets familiar with the sensation of moving that much faster. You learn to stay on top of that speed and then stay that fast.

This is the kind of training exercise I'll do midseason. I usually go through a pretty varied training regimen, working three-week blocks of programming. Through that time, I'll be working out six days a week—six days on the track, with two or three of those days also including a session in the weight room. We'll go very hard one week, semi-hard the next, and then follow that with an easier week. That's the idea anyway. Really, to me they all feel pretty hard.

Well before the outdoor competition season begins, we focus

on the foundation of my fitness. Just as with a house, that base has to be rock solid. Without it, my body won't be able to endure the rigours of a long season. These sessions aren't as intense as the ones I'll do in the spring and summer when I'm sharpening my speed, but the volume is higher. We do longer interval sessions, running hills or stadium stairs. I spend a lot of time in the weight room, building my strength—with a key focus on my core. I'll also do technical drills to optimize my stride pattern and find my rhythm before we progress to any all-out sprint sessions.

I'm not moving at full speed yet. It's not time to run super fast. That comes gradually. First you need to build a block of fitness. The human body isn't built to run as fast as sprinters do all the time. It will break down if I try—and I'll get injured. Everything has got to be precise. It has to be timed. I can't just get right into it after taking necessary time off. Basically, I'm out of shape—at least, out of shape for an Olympic sprinter. I think of it as like my "track shape," but obviously I'm not out of shape in relation to most people. I still run in the off-season. I stay as active as possible doing other sports and activities, like cross-training and basket-ball. I always need to keep my body conditioned.

But I've got to build back to my peak level of fitness, and that doesn't happen overnight. So for the first little while, I'm just like a regular runner, until I can work my way into a condition where I can ramp up the speed. For the first three months of an off-season, I'm not even wearing spikes; I'm just in running shoes. I'll train in my flats (as we call them), sprinting up stadium stairs or hills, just trying to build a foundation. My weight training during this time focuses on building back my strength, doing a lot of core exercises and conditioning.

At the same time, I go through a sort of mental reset. I have to recalibrate my mind, my body, my soul—everything. You need to build up the confidence and will to push through the pain of building back to where you were. You need to tell yourself it's all right, it's a new year, and it's time to get better. It's time to put in that work again.

The "starting over" is the hard part—probably the hardest in any given season—because every year is so different. It takes a long time to get back to where you left off. Some days I'll finish a long day at the track and feel demoralized.

The same kind of training felt so easy last year. Why is it so hard now? As the years go by, all that extra mileage starts to catch up on me. Every year, it gets a little bit harder.

"You've got to do this all over again," I tell myself. "You've got to figure this out."

There is no time to rest on the success of last season, or to dwell on any failures. You have to build back and move forward. You need to work your ass off to regain that speed you know you're capable of. There is only one direction to go.

But it takes months to get there. It takes time to feel like you can compete at the level you did before. And that's if you're relatively healthy. Overcoming an injury creates a whole other degree of pain.

There are times when you almost want to quit. There are times when you wonder whether you'll reach the heights you reached before. But that's the thing about peaks—they are always followed by valleys. Those valleys are necessary to regroup, rebuild, and relaunch.

You've got to begin again. That's true in so many areas of life when you're looking for success. Once you've achieved something, the next task awaits. I believe it's important to step back and assess how to best chase after your next goals. In sprinting, that requires rest and rebuilding. The process might look a little different depending on your field or your goals, but the underlying principle is the same.

Eventually, as the training continues, I'll put on the spikes that I race in. They're super light, with a stiff plate at the bottom to return as much energy as possible. But running in spikes takes a lot more out of your body than using regular running shoes. Part of that is because an elite sprinter will typically apply a peak force of about five times their body weight to the track surface beneath them each step. By comparison, if an average person were to sprint, they would typically apply one and a half to two times their body weight per step.

Usually around the start of the New Year, we start to do a little bit of work in spikes, but not every day. My coach will basically say, "I want you to go faster now. I want you to come through at this time." I'll start to feel the speed coming back. I'll find the confidence I carried the season before and know I can be better than my previous best.

I'll remember that success comes from preparation—and that often the preparation is the hardest part. But it's all part of the same, constant process.

Even when I'm on vacation or taking some time to rest after a long season, it's all part of being ready for what comes next. There's that saying if you want to be ready, you've got to stay ready.

That mantra has connected with me. While I'm not always in peak condition to race, I'm never not thinking about the path back to getting into that state. It's a cycle, which means it keeps moving.

That's the kind of attitude I have, no matter what I'm doing: I stay ready at all times. I don't need to *get* ready—because I'm *always* ready.

13

KNOW YOUR VALUE

What would it take for you to leave school and go pro?"

When I was first asked that question, I had no idea what to say. It was something I'd never considered before. I was only 20 years old and was still processing the dizzying speed with which I'd become a rising star on the track. It was 2015, and I'd just won the NCAA 100-metre and 200-metre titles with USC.

Instead of being an exciting time, it was stressful and overwhelming. Agents started to call my mom constantly, trying to convince her to get me to sign with them.

There were potentially lucrative opportunities for me to drop out of USC, sign an endorsement deal, and go pro. Back then, an NCAA athlete wasn't allowed to accept any kind of sponsorship deal and remain eligible for competition. If you tried to make money off your ability, you were considered ineligible.

Mom had never been in this situation before, and she was trying her best to help me navigate my life. One of the many agents who reached out to her was Brian Levine, a Toronto-based agent who specializes in marketing for athletes. He'd end up being a trusted part of my inner circle—but at the time my mother didn't know what to make of him. He was just another voice among the many trying to get a piece of her son. Always protective, she decided to just not tell me about the agents. She wanted me to focus on my education and on doing well in the upcoming Pan American Games in Toronto and the World Championships in Beijing in August 2015.

She wasn't able to keep everyone away though. After I nearly beat Bolt in Beijing, the conversation became impossible to ignore. My mom was in Beijing and met with my eventual track agent, Paul Doyle, in a hotel lobby to talk about what was possible. Suddenly, it seemed like everyone was in my ear. There was pressure to stay in school and keep running for a track program that had given me a dream opportunity. And there were others telling me I was crazy for considering it. This was finally my chance to cash in, they said. Some people told me, "Do what is best for you"—but as a 20-year-old kid, how are you supposed to be sure?

Going pro meant leaving my coach, Caryl Smith Gilbert, even though we'd had so much success together.

I loved Caryl. I had so much respect for her. During my time at USC, Caryl and Quincy Watts took my talent and turned me into a double-gold national champion in both the 100 and 200. I went on to win bronze in both the 100 metres and 4 x 100 metres at the 2015 World Championships in Beijing. That season I became just the third Canadian to legally break the 10-second barrier in the 100 metres, behind Donovan Bailey and Bruny Surin.

Things were going very well. To everyone around me, it seemed like my career was taking off.

So why mess with something that was working?

But I had raced 54 times during the previous year, which was basically double what many would consider a lot. I was exhausted and running on fumes. I knew I needed rest and a new direction if I was going to reach the podium at the Rio Olympics in 2016. Very few athletes are able to run an entire NCAA season and then get onto the podium at a World Championships or Olympics, which are typically held at least 6 to 10 weeks after the NCAA championship.

It was a tough call.

One day I was introduced to Andrew Maulseed, who had some connections to shoe sponsors. Andrew asked me directly: "What would it take for you to leave school and go pro?"

I had no idea what to say, so I threw out a number I thought was wild. I had enough information at the time to know that super lucrative contracts in track were rare. What the hell, I thought— let's go big:

"A million dollars," I said.

There was no way . . .

"Okay," Andrew replied. "I'm going to see if that's possible and I'll call you back tomorrow."

Sure enough, he called me back the next day. He told me he'd spoken with the main guy at Puma who oversees the track athletes they sign, and he could offer me a million dollars to leave USC, turn pro, and start representing their brand in competition. I could get paid by Puma just for wearing their footwear and apparel and also make money from the organizers putting on the meets.

"*Whoa,*" I thought. That was a lot of money.

But was it real? At 20 years old I still had no idea who I should trust. The situation made me incredibly uncomfortable, almost nervous. I didn't want to make a fool of myself. I also didn't want to miss out on that kind of money. And I didn't want to abandon USC—or the free education I was receiving there.

What would I say to my college coach? How would I tell Caryl I wanted to leave USC after what we'd accomplished?

I was proud of everything we'd accomplished at USC. I was proud to be the national champion. I was astonished by what we'd achieved and knew I couldn't have done it without Caryl and Quincy. I'd always be grateful. But maybe it was time for the next chapter.

But I still I didn't know what to do. So naturally, I told my mom about the offer.

"Don't be naive," she said. "You don't know who this guy is. You don't know what his intentions are."

So I went back to Andrew, still in disbelief, and asked if I could speak with the person from Puma who had made the offer. Andrew agreed to set up a video conference call. I'd looked the guy up on Google to make sure he even existed. Sure enough, he did—and when I saw that his face matched the man I'd googled, I knew it was real. He asked if it was true that I was interested in leaving USC, signing an endorsement deal, and turning pro. I told him I was considering it.

"Is that possible?" I asked.

"Yes, of course," he said. "We can make that work. Who is your agent?"

I didn't know what to say. At that point I didn't even realize I should *have* an agent.

"Shit," I remember thinking. "This is *real*. A *million* dollars. I can actually get this money."

I had to go find myself an agent!

I called my mom to tell her it was all true. I met the guy myself—it was really him.

"Okay," she said. "Well, that's a lot of money."

Whatever decision you make, my mother told me, just be happy about it—but only if I promised I would finish my university degree regardless.

"This is a prestigious school," she said. "You need something to fall back on."

Track is not like the NBA or the NHL, she reminded me. Nothing is guaranteed. If I suffered an injury as a pro basketball player, I'd still have 10 to 20 million to carry me into retirement. But a million dollars would only stretch so far. It's great, but it won't guarantee long-term wealth.

I vowed to my mother that if I went pro, I would finish my degree.

That's when I finally learned that dozens of agents had already been trying to reach out to her. I dove into my research, looking up the names on the list she gave me. At first, I didn't find any that gave me a good vibe. I've always been pretty intuitive in feeling people out. Often people think I'm just quiet, but really I like to listen and observe. I want to know someone's motivation before I agree to work with them.

Paul Doyle, whom my mom had already met with in Beijing,

was one of the only agents who stood out. He had a stellar roster of athletes, including Asafa Powell, the Jamaican 100-metre sprinter, who broke the world record twice, and Ashton Eaton, the two-time Olympic champion in decathlon who held the world record in the event for a number of years. And when I spoke to him, he was immediately open about the perils of working with an agent. A lot of them were in it only for themselves, he said. "You have to be very careful," he said. I felt like I could trust Paul.

He told me he uses a special software program with his athletes that allows them to see all the money that comes through winnings and endorsement and where it all goes. You could see all the transactions, like a bank account. It was a completely transparent process. None of the other agents I interviewed had something like that.

After I decided to work with Paul, he told me he wanted to wait on Puma's initial offer and explore the market. As a 20-year-old, I was unsure about passing up such a large sum of money. But I had faith in Paul's experience.

Before I made my decision public, rumours that I was thinking of going pro started to spread. I faced a lot of criticism for it from the NCAA track community. It looked like I was selling out for a payday.

But I ignored what the critics said. I had to block them out. In doubting my decisions, they put negativity on me. They were basically saying they didn't trust my judgment, or the decisions I made about my own career.

These were my dreams. I had to accomplish them my way.

My mother was a huge support through this. She reminded me that it was my decision and that I needed to do what felt best for me. You live and die by your decisions, she told me, so you need to believe in the choices you make. If there are consequences, you'll live with them—but they will belong to you, because you are in charge of your own decisions.

With Paul at the helm, we spoke with Adidas, which came in with an offer that topped Puma's initial proposal. We also spoke with New Balance, which had already signed Trayvon Bromell, whom I tied with for bronze at the 2015 World Athletics Championships. Paul figured out what he'd been offered, which set a new bar for our expectations in all our conversations.

When Paul approached Nike, they came back with an even larger offer and invited me to the Nike headquarters in Portland, Oregon, to sit down and discuss their pitch.

We flew to Portland with Paul and my mom. Nike blew me away. The headquarters are state of the art, like nothing I'd ever seen before. They have buildings named for the greatest athletes in the world that they've endorsed, the Michael Jordan Building and the Tiger Woods Building. I'd just turned 21 years old right before the trip. They gave me a card that allowed me to buy whatever I wanted from the Nike store on site. "Whatever you can't take with you, we'll ship to you," I was told. It was close to Christmas, so I ended up buying so much stuff for my family back home. I kept the receipt. The final bill was more than $10,000!

On the sign above the conference room where Nike executives presented to us, there was an image of the tattoo of my last name that I have across my back. Inside they'd posted quotes that I said in prior media interviews. They had shirts printed with the slogan "De Grasse Knows Fast," mirroring their classic "Bo Knows . . ." campaign with Bo Jackson from the '90s, and laid out a potential marketing campaign. They gave me customized shoes with an ADG logo printed on the side and a pair of brand new Air Force Ones. It was an incredible presentation; I'd never seen anything like it before. (I still have the shoes and gear they gave me.)

We were in town for two days. I took a tour of the facility on the second day, visiting the Michael Jordan Building. It was unreal.

My mom was sold right off the bat. Nike wanted me to sign right there. I remember walking down a hall with her when she whispered, "You have to sign with them!" I was pretty much ready to sign too. But I knew this wasn't my area of expertise. I'd put my trust in Paul.

He told me to enjoy the moment and have fun, but that we still needed to wait for other companies to get back to us. It was a difficult lesson. I was so enamoured with the Nike gear I'd shipped home for cousins and friends that I was ready to sign my name. As a 21-year-old, just being there felt like a dream. I was all in: "Just do it!" I told myself.

I could have just become a Nike athlete right then and there.

But Paul had bigger plans. This wasn't his first trip to Nike headquarters, and he was determined to get me the best deal possible. After we left Portland, Paul circled back to Puma, which is based in Germany—a much longer trip than a couple days in Oregon. Instead of having us travel to Europe, Puma sent us several packages of prototypes for shoes and gear. With Nike and Adidas in the mix, we had leverage I hadn't understood I had before.

In the end, despite all the bells and whistles of Nike's pitch, Puma returned with the best offer.

It was much more than I'd initially been offered. Had I jumped the gun, I would have taken the very first proposal we'd received.

To a young guy like me, that initial offer seemed unthinkable. But the fear and uncertainty I felt right away was a powerful instinct. It was something that, I can see now, I learned from my mother. In her protective nature, she kept the distraction of dollar signs and lofty promises by potential agents out of my head. Her skepticism of how the initial Puma offer materialized challenged me to be careful about making a quick decision without considering all the angles. At the time, I wasn't equipped to see them. I was blind to so much.

When we chase success, sometimes we can lose sight of wisdom. There are many areas in our lives where we might be tempted by the first offer that comes along or feel pressured into acting without considering the other potential outcomes. At Nike, I was ready to sign on the line after a fancy presentation and a whole bunch of free gear. In the end, though, I followed Paul's calm and confident approach to the negotiation. The transition of turning pro taught me the importance of knowing my worth. I believe that lesson can apply to many areas in your own pursuit of success. It might be a conversation about a job, a salary negotiation, a business deal, or any other of myriad situations in which its crucial to know the hand you hold. Do the work to find out what you're worth, and have the confidence to ask for it. You owe that much to yourself.

14

GOOD ON GAS

Y ou probably want a car, right?" Paul Doyle asked me the day I signed my contract with Puma in 2016.

Visions of Lamborghinis and Mercedes revved in my head.

"Well, I suggest right now we go to the dealership and we get you a Honda," Paul said. "They are great on gas—and the cars last a long time. Honda or maybe a Toyota."

I had never owned a car before. I didn't even know how the process of buying a car worked. We went straight to the Honda dealership in Los Angeles that day. We looked at a couple Civics and some Accords. I test-drove a few different models.

"What do you think?" Paul asked me.

It was nice, but it was no McLaren.

"Well," I shrugged. "I mean, it's okay . . ."

"Start out with this," Paul said. "Trust me, it will be worth it."

But I didn't even have any money yet. Paul had to front me the money to buy me the Accord, and I paid him back out of my first cheque from Puma.

By contract, I suddenly had more money than I'd ever thought possible. But in reality, that money didn't exist yet. It was a huge deal, but I still had to earn that money over several years. It would actually become just one of many corporate partnerships that would allow me to build wealth as an athlete.

As a young man, I didn't have a concept of viewing the big picture in regard to my finances yet. But the day I signed that contract, Paul was very direct with me.

"You need to be smart with this," he said. "I've seen too many athletes blow this."

It was an indispensable lesson for me. I could have celebrated the Puma deal by blowing a bunch of cash and acting like a fool. But Paul was very clear. He didn't want to see me make those kinds of mistakes. He told me how important it was to focus on saving my money and managing it well. He connected me with a financial advisor who works with professional athletes and encouraged me to interview several more, so that I was able to find the right connection with someone who could help me plan out my future financial goals.

I drove that Accord for the next five years, travelling around Phoenix while training with Stuart McMillan. When I moved to Florida, I drove it across the country. A couple years ago, I traded in that first Accord for a new one, and I still drive a Honda today.

It's not that I don't enjoy fancier things. I recently bought a Tesla, which I keep along with the Accord. But everyone I love has a better car than I do. I bought my girlfriend Nia a Mercedes and my mother a BMW. Of course, I get to drive both of those here and there. And I have my eye on one of those new Tesla Cybertrucks.

But at my core, I'm still a Honda guy. Like Paul said, it's great on gas and it lasts. It's also kind of a symbol of me. It's a reminder that I need to be careful about how I spend my money and that I need to keep the bigger picture in mind.

I've been blessed to be able to do many things I never thought possible. I was able to help my mother retire and to buy her a new house.

Because of my busy schedule, I'll sometimes take a private jet when I need to zip across the country or back to Canada to do a commercial shoot or appear at an event. But that's an expense related to time management more than indulgence—and the cost is always factored into the overall fee of what I'll earn by making the trip. Other times, I can be comically frugal, like making sure a $15 wire transfer fee is covered when I'm sent money from my agent for an appearance. Every dollar counts. I've been cognizant of that from the start.

That was the hard part, coming up as a kid. I learned quickly, through the guidance of people like Paul, that even though it seemed like I was living a dream I was also in a vulnerable position. There are way too many examples out there of someone coming into a lot of money one day, and just like that, they have no idea where it went. They don't realize it doesn't matter how much money is coming in, you have to budget it. You can't go crazy. You need to make it last. A salary is paid out over a year, so you need to keep the small, daily, weekly, monthly picture in mind. You have to pay taxes and fees, which means as much as half that money isn't even yours.

One of the first corporate partnerships my marketing agent Brian landed for me was with a global accounting firm. I visited their headquarters in Toronto and got a real education. I was able to learn about how to budget, save on my taxes, and set up my own business and eventually my charitable foundation. That was definitely an unexpected perk and benefit of that sponsorship.

When I started to understand the value in this kind of an education, I also realized how many athletes—and young people—don't do this stuff. They seemed surprised when I told them about different techniques for wealth management that I'd learned. And I was surprised by how little they knew. It wasn't their fault. Nobody had told them. It's not something you learn in high school. Most of us learn by making mistakes. Just as I listen to trusted advice about my physical well-being and performance, I listen to the best advice I can get on how to handle my finances.

If I can offer some wisdom from what I've learned about finances, it's that regardless of how much money you make, you need to be careful with how you use what you earn and diligent about managing with the future in mind.

It goes beyond saving money and investing it wisely though. I'm amazed at some of the talented Olympic athletes who don't do their due diligence in putting together the optimal management team to guide them and enhance their earning potential. It's a big issue in track in particular.

My needs and goals today are much different from what they were just a few years ago. I'm a father now. My kids depend on me to provide for them, not only each day but also to allow them to have a comfortable life. What will life be like for them if something were to happen to me? (You never actually think about life insurance until you're a parent. Suddenly you don't feel quite so immortal.) Even though I've managed to make a decent amount of money in my career, I have to keep the totality of my needs in perspective.

I think about how hard my mother had to work to make sure I had everything I needed in life. I remember how expensive it was to get what so many other people took for granted, like a laptop to study at Coffeyville. I was learning lessons back then too. My mother was setting me up to value what I have and the work it takes to earn it. I value every dollar I make because of the example she gave me. And through the challenges of my hamstring injury and the COVID pandemic, I learned how quickly those paycheques can stop.

Setting yourself up to reach your goals and achieve success means taking care of all areas of your life. You don't need to make millions to learn that lesson. Far too many people—especially young people—overlook their financial health. Whatever you earn, whatever you've saved, be proud of it. If you're struggling financially, it's okay. You're not alone. I know what that grind is like too. Don't focus on the frivolous things you don't have. Think about how you can best position yourself for future financial success, even if that means sacrifice now. Respect every dollar you make. You earned it.

15

ACT LIKE A PRO

I t took me a while to learn how to be a pro. Early on in my career, I took for granted the level of commitment that was required of me.

Before the Olympics I shot a pizza commercial and was featured in an ad campaign for Gillette. The pizza commercial was a little cheesy (pun intended), but it was fun to be on TV ahead of the Games. The Gillette sponsorship was interesting. Obviously, it's an amazing brand. But there was a clause in the contract that I had to remain clean shaven. However, I didn't want to be lining up next to guys like Bolt and Gatlin with my little baby face. So my marketing agent had to call up Gillette and explain that we needed to amend the agreement to allow me to sport a chin strap beard. They agreed, and while I'm not certain how much faster I ran as a result, I know I felt more confident lining up against those older men.

It wasn't until after Rio, with my increased profile, that the sponsorship and magazine cover opportunities started to build up. Right away it seemed like every weekend I was on a plane to another event or commercial shoot.

I enjoyed a lot of it. I went to Chile to open a new Puma store. I was given a tour of schools and attended some track events where we gave away shoes. The kids loved me. I was surprised to learn they actually knew who I was. We did a photo shoot and I signed autographs. Then I cut the ribbon to open up the new store in Santiago. I enjoyed the trip so much that I volunteered to do another. The next year they sent me to do the same thing in Mexico City.

But it wasn't always fun stuff like that. Often the marketing commitments I had with brands felt like a chore.

My marketing agent, Brian, worked diligently to find opportunities to help build my brand. He would set up an event or a campaign shoot with one of my partners, but I'd let him know it wasn't something I wanted to do.

I didn't understand how significant those relationships were back then. I didn't grasp the importance of building my own brand and developing a strong and lasting bond with corporate partners and the platform that would give me down the road. I didn't realize that one opportunity can lead to more opportunities. It wasn't just about the present. I had to position myself for the future too.

If someone wants to make a living as a track and field athlete, they have to hustle. You don't receive a salary like you do if you are playing pro basketball or baseball, and you aren't going to make a living off earnings from winnings at track meets alone. You might land a lucrative contract with a shoe company, if you're lucky. But that comes with many responsibilities, targets, and obligations.

Brian tried to show me how important that hustle was, especially early on. If a track athlete wants to avoid the spotlight and just compete, it's pretty easy to disappear. But if they want to earn a living doing what they love, they need to be visible and appealing. They need to put themselves out there. It's much different than being an NBA player who is on TV three to four times a week.

Despite Brian's best efforts, it took me a while to figure that out.

After Rio, he encouraged me to do as many interviews as possible, to keep the momentum going. The equation was simple: the more interviews you do, the more exposure you get, the more popularity you gain, the more appealing you are to brands, the more contracts you land, the more money you make. It was like a brand-building snowball effect. And while I enjoyed a lot of it, it grew tiresome.

"Man, I've done enough interviews," I told Brian after one long press junket. "I've got a headache!"

It was a lot for an introvert. I found it exhausting and didn't love talking about myself all the time. I still had to break out of my shell. Brian understood but kept encouraging me, knowing it was in my best interest to build upon the success of the Rio Olympics and the profile I had quickly created for myself.

I was a young man and all of a sudden, everybody was paying attention to me. I wasn't even 22 yet. I'd never experienced this and never thought anything like this could happen in my life.

And there was a good side to that, obviously. It was cool to see my face on a billboard at Yonge-Dundas Square in downtown Toronto. But at the same time, that puts a lot of pressure on you.

With Usain Bolt nearing the end of his career, Puma wanted me to be the new face of track.

"Damn, I just *started* track," I thought.

Everything was happening so quickly.

With all that exposure, you need to be careful about everything you say and do in public. You have to be mindful where you go—always being aware of anything that could potentially reflect negatively on you and damage your image.

Long before I was a track star, I was an immature kid who said and did a lot of the dumb things that immature young people do. After winning silver in the 200 metres in Rio, someone scrolled through my old social media posts from high school and found a past reference to smoking pot and rap lyrics that some might find offensive. After receiving a call from the head of communications at Athletics Canada, Brian called me in a panic but couldn't reach me. But one of my friends had access to my social media accounts and spent hours going through my old posts to clear out all traces of my juvenile behaviour. I was so fortunate to have people in my corner to protect me from my past self.

I also had to learn some hard lessons about how to act professionally in honouring my commitments.

One morning I showed up to a commercial shoot an hour late. I didn't think it really mattered, even though there was a 50-person production crew waiting for me. My lateness threw the schedule off for the entire day. It was incredibly disrespectful of their time. But I didn't see that back then. To me, it was just another demand on my time, and it seemed like a burden. I didn't care about it.

Brian pulled me aside and told me I needed to do better.

"This is a big deal," he told me. "It's Gatorade!"

It was about more than just a delayed shoot. It was about the effect that had on how people viewed me. It was about my reputation as a professional.

At the time, I brushed Brian off. I didn't understand why he was so upset. I'd like to say I learned my lesson right there—but I was late for a few more commitments after that. It was a problem, but I was too immature to see it. (For the record, I turned things around with Gatorade, and they remain one of my most loyal partners to this day.)

It took me at least a couple of years to realize the necessity of showing up and being professional, regardless of how tired I was or how inconsequential I might think the event or commitment was. I wasn't entitled to the sponsorship I was getting. There is never an obligation for a brand to renew its partnership with me if it no longer sees value in what I bring—or if, frankly, I'm too much of a headache to work with. By being irresponsible and dismissive, I was jeopardizing everything I was trying to build.

That lesson really set in for me when I first went through my hamstring injury in 2017 and I finally understood just how quicky the interest in me could fade away. One second you're on top and the next thing you know, you're down. That was a humbling lesson to learn.

As I matured and grew as a professional, I learned to take those obligations much more seriously. I showed up on time. I started to make sure I made connections with people on the set of commercials and that I was putting the best version of myself out there. I realized every interaction I have has an impact, and there is a ripple effect.

I learned the importance of communicating and mingling. I've learned that you've got to make that appearance, even if you're not in the best mood. You have to put on your big boy pants and show up to work on time.

I'm fortunate to have the brand partnerships that I do. Companies like Gatorade and Puma have been with me from the start. Other opportunities have allowed me to expand my reach and polish my presentation skills—and even expand into creative places. So many opportunities have come through the corporate relationships I've been fortunate to build.

I've chatted onstage with bank executives. I've spoken about the importance of mental health with the innovative wellness company headversity. I've appeared on massive billboards for Gatorade. I've enjoyed coming up with funny lines in commercials for Subway. I've tried my hand at acting, with a cameo in the TV show *Murdoch Mysteries*, dressing up as a store owner from a century ago and chasing down a thief.

I've even run through a wall and trekked through a hurricane for GoDaddy.

"I'm Andre De Grasse, and I believe in being unstoppable," I said in that commercial, sitting on a bench in a locker room.

Then I got up and ran directly through the wall beside me. On TV, it looks like a clean break. But I insisted on doing the stunt myself and it took a couple takes. The first time I didn't run straight through the wall and toppled over into the material that was meant to break apart. I ended up on the floor with my feet dangling over the fake brick wall. My management team was watching with the client and the rest of the crew. It was dead silent until I got back on my feet. Then everyone burst into laughter. But Brian and Nic thought for a moment I had injured myself a mere two months ahead of the Olympics. And I'd already taken a bit of a risk by flying up to Toronto to shoot this commercial in the middle of a pandemic. But I loved every second of it and I was never in any danger, because the wall was made of foam blocks. The next take I blasted right through like a superhero.

Later in the same commercial shoot, I trudged through a simulated hurricane. It was a very chilly spring day, and I was facing a wind machine with water blasting into my face.

"Don't stop being unstoppable, Canada," I said into the camera, shielding myself from the fake rain with my arm.

"We've got enough footage," Brian told the director. "Andre is soaking wet and shivering. He needs to be back at practice in Florida tomorrow. Time to shut this down!"

The client from GoDaddy agreed with Brian, and I was given some towels and a fresh set of clothes. But the whole experience was a blast.

I'm lucky to have had the opportunity to grow as a professional—and grateful that some of those early moments where I lacked awareness and maturity didn't ruin the opportunities I value so much today. I now know how fortunate I am. My deal with Puma is only part of a wide range of endorsements and partnerships that are vital to my brand. They are a fundamental part of my career and the financial stability I am building for my family's future.

How you carry yourself matters. That's one of the key things I've learned in my career. My job is about much more than running fast and winning races. That's the foundation, of course— that's why people pay attention. But being a professional requires more than reaching the podium.

It's valuable to remember that in all areas of life. The impression we make defines who we are to others. And if you want to make a lasting impression, you need to show people that you value their time and that you take your commitments seriously. I believe I've been able to create lasting relationships with corporate sponsors because when I show up, I put in the work—just like I would on the track. I make sure that people know I'm happy to be there and that I value what they do. When that lesson finally clicked for me, that's when I became a true pro.

16

KNOW YOURSELF

When making a big decision about the direction you are heading in pursuit of your goals, prepare a plan that works for you.

This requires understanding yourself and how you learn. It requires reflecting on what has worked before and what hasn't.

If you have a specific goal in mind, you will need a path to follow that is specific to you. Every approach is different. It can't be uniform. It's got to be somewhat unique and tailored to your needs.

Today, I trust my instincts because I've worked with countless people, trying to improve in any way I can throughout my career.

Some athletes like to have a lot of control over the plan their coach lays out for them. That's not my style.

I hire a coach to be the expert at what they do, so that I can get better at what I do. I have to trust their expertise; I have to trust in the reason I hired them in the first place. At the same time, I've changed coaches through my career more than most sprinters do. I believe it's important to be able to discern when something just isn't working out. I put faith in my coach and stick to their plan, as long as their plan is working. But as I adapt as an athlete and as the circumstances around what I need as an athlete change, I trust my instinct and make a difficult, but necessary, change.

I rely on my coach to lay out a training plan. Some athletes are deeply involved in programming their training regimen, but I'm not the type of athlete who overthinks that too much. As long as things are working and I'm progressing, I'm happy. I've had several different kinds of coaches over the years, each with a different approach. I think each has had the kind of style I needed at a given point in my career.

My first coach, Tony Sharpe, would tell me everything we were doing before we started each day. He explained the plan thoroughly, making sure I not only knew what we were doing in practice but also understood why we were doing it. I was just starting out in track at the time, so this was an effective approach. It helped me understand why we were preparing a certain way and how it would help me perform better. Tony broke the art of sprinting down for me so I could better understand what we were trying to achieve and how to get there.

Later on, I had coaches who took more of a need-to-know approach. Coach Caryl at USC told me only what she felt I had to know. She turned me into an NCAA champion in the 100 and 200. During training, Caryl would tell me to do something and I'd do it. No questions asked; no argument given. She knew what she was doing, and what she was doing was guiding me on my way to becoming the national champ.

Stuart McMillan, the first coach I had when I went pro, had everything planned out well in advance. He would send me emails every Sunday, mapping out everything we'd be working on that week in detail. For him, week by week was the best way to prepare me. That helped me look ahead and realize just how much work I had to put in. It was his way of ensuring I was able to balance my life on and off the track. With everything laid out, I knew how to prepare for my workouts each day. I had to make sure I was on top of things. For example, if there was going to be a particularly tough workout, I knew I'd need to skip going out and get extra sleep the night before. I was able to be focused and locked in.

My next coach, Rana Reider, would never tell me what we were working on beforehand. I'd show up at the track and find out what the workout was right then and there. I think there was some value to that approach as well. It allowed me to leave my work at the track and trust in the process my coach was implementing. That would drive some athletes crazy. Others might like that approach more than receiving a bunch of information from their coach every week.

I've had success with all those approaches, so I don't have a strong preference. I let my coaches be comfortable in what works for them. There isn't a single approach to coaching or planning that works for everyone, just as there isn't a single approach to leading or managing. We each need to decide what works best for us. But there has to be a connection between everyone involved—an understanding of how things are going to work and complete buy-in of that process, right down to how and when competition and travel schedules are agreed to.

However my coach approaches the programming for my training, I always work within that system in my own way. For example, you eventually become familiar with how your coach operates and get a sense of where your workouts are going. I write down my thoughts on each workout, recording what works well for me and what doesn't. When it seems like a particular workout hasn't been effective, I bring the issue up with my coach. I'll let them know I don't feel it's been beneficial to my progress. This is something I've started to do later in my career. Early on, when I was still fresh, I found it hard to inject my own perspective. I was just there to learn. But now I'm an expert too—and I know my body better than anyone. My coaches absolutely know what they are doing, but my feedback helps them better understand whether it's working the way they intended. We come to a compromise, based on each perspective, and come up with an effective plan, based on that input.

A key part of preparation is knowing your body and knowing yourself—understanding how you operate and how you get the best results. When you are looking for a coach, or a training plan—or whatever kind of system you need to help you improve—find someone or something that fits with those specific realities about who you are and how you work. It's definitely a balance between being open to learning from the expertise of others and being aware of what you need.

A coach might give you a workout, but they don't know how you feel after it. You need to give them feedback. You have to know the difference between the discomfort of a hard workout and the pain of a potentially damaging one. A good coach will see that something that is working for one of their athletes might not be for another. In my case, I want a coach to find the best way of getting me back to running as quickly as possible. I don't have time for setbacks, so I want them to adjust my routine with the goal of achieving my peak speed.

As the year goes on, you figure out the plan. You have a sense of what's coming next, based on what you've done over the past few weeks. For example, I know that Monday we'll focus on my starts and acceleration, while on Tuesday we'll do longer runs (which we call tempo runs). I keep track of what we're working on, writing down notes after each training session, trying to keep a record I can follow. It allows me to reflect on the effectiveness of the process. I'm always trying to figure out the dynamics of what is working and what isn't with a coach.

As much as I trust in my coach's plan, I want to be able to see where I'm progressing and where that progress is starting to slow. In the end, the results fall on me—so I have a responsibility to be active and purposeful in my approach to training.

In track, it can be challenging to find the right fit because your coach is often working with a group of athletes, not just you. That happens in other sports too, of course. That's the reality in any team sport, even if there are coaches who specialize in specific positions. In those situations it's easy for an athlete's individual needs to get lost. That's a problem.

I've witnessed some situations where a coach will give each of the athletes they are working with the same program, and whoever does well with it has success—and whoever doesn't, doesn't.

But the opposite can be an issue too. There are situations

where it can feel like certain athletes are getting more attention than others. It can be perceived as favouritism, and it can create tension and jealousy within the group.

Both of those situations are detrimental to development.

The approaches aren't designed with each athlete's unique circumstances or best interests in mind. A good coach will adapt their plans based on the input of their athlete, because every athlete is different. Something that works for one athlete might not work for another. That's what makes a good coach—a good teacher, a good leader—the ability to adapt their approach depending on the needs of the person they are working with.

There are other situations where athletes working in a group might not like that another athlete is doing something different from them. They might feel like they're getting left out, or that their coach is not doing a good job with them because they are making them do one thing, while someone else does a different routine. But some things work for some athletes and some things don't.

A good coach knows how to show each of their athletes that they have their specific needs in mind.

If you're in a position where you're seeking that kind of support, do what you can to find the kind of coach who is adaptable and capable of knowing exactly what you need in order to achieve your best.

Finding the right fit in your growth is a key part of achieving success. In my situation, that means finding the right coach. But this applies to many areas of life, where someone requires the guidance of a leader to help them achieve their goals. Maybe it's a teacher. Maybe it's a boss. Maybe it's a parent or a mentor. If you're in a position to help guide people towards their goals, I think it's important that you keep their perspectives in mind.

Good instruction relies on adaptability. There is no uniform way to get the best out of all people. We're all different—and we all learn, find motivation, and are inspired in different ways.

17

NOTHING PERSONAL

My goal heading into the Tokyo Olympics in the summer of 2021 was clear: I planned to win three gold medals. I wrote it down. I told my coaches. I told everybody in my inner circle.

"That's my goal," I said. "I want to leave Tokyo with three Olympic gold medals."

I'd won three Olympic medals in Rio. As proud as I was of what I'd accomplished in Rio, in Tokyo I planned to surpass that.

That might sound overly confident, but it wasn't that I felt I could easily win three gold medals. I knew every other man running beside me had the same goal in mind, and I knew each of them, on any given day, was fast enough to do it. I knew very well it wasn't going to be easy. Especially because I was entered in three events, and none of the other top sprinters were doing that.

But I spoke that goal out loud and wrote it down because I wanted to be accountable to it. I spoke that expectation into existence. Three gold medals was the standard of excellence I wanted to achieve.

My previous success was in the past and now I wanted to surpass it. It was about setting a new target, as difficult as it was.

It's not very hard to find parallels between sprinting and life. It's why so many colloquial sayings come from the sport. A foot race is one of the purest physical tests there is. As I've said, it's really just you versus you.

If you think about it, that's true of most goals we set out to achieve in life. The people you are competing with matter, of course. To them, you're just as much an obstacle to your goals as you are to theirs. And you want to be the best. You want to stand on top of the podium and celebrate a win. That requires beating everyone else. But in track you have no control over what others do. It's not like basketball or hockey, where you can play defence and affect the outcome of a game. As a sprinter, you need to stay in your lane. It's a raw test of power and speed, measured by what your body alone is capable of.

But if you focus on surpassing your past achievements rather than worrying about what and how others are doing, you'll find you can narrow your attention to the improvements you can make in your own performance.

I find inspiration in so many other athletes. But I've always admired athletes who have mastered individual greatness—like Serena Williams and Tiger Woods, who both carved out untouchable legacies with their sheer dominance. Serena changed tennis. Tiger changed golf. They both literally redefined their sports. I think of Kobe Bryant the same way. When I was growing up, Kobe set the standard for how basketball was played. So many players on the court during his career and after have tried to emulate him in some way, just like Michael Jordan before him. Kobe's "mamba mentality" is a guiding force for me. This was a man who could score 45 points and practise into the early morning after a game because he felt he needed the work.

There are only a few athletes who come along and have that kind of impact. I think they all share a pursuit of personal excellence that is uncommon. The greats dominate their sports not just because they beat everyone else, but also because they are constantly trying to do better than their previous best. They were never fully satisfied with their performances, because even their biggest successes would set a new height to conquer.

When it comes to competition, one of the mantras I live by on the track is "nothing personal." The concept came up during a chat I had with Anson Henry. A couple of years ago, he told me he wanted to see more edge from me—a bit more flair, like I carried when I was younger and first emerged on the scene beating people I wasn't supposed to.

Anson was right. I certainly carried much more swagger then than I do today, but I was much more insecure than I let on. I think it was because I arrived on the scene so unexpectedly. Nobody was more shocked by my early success in track than I was. The idea of being a track star hadn't crossed my mind until Tony told me he believed I could be something special. It took a lot of convincing for me to actually believe that too.

Even after I turned professional, I'd watch other guys run and be amazed at how fast they were. I'd let their times get into my head. I was still learning what I was capable of and still grappling with the reality that I was among the fastest people in the world. When I'd see results from meets I didn't attend, I'd feel discouraged by news of a blistering race run by one of my competitors. "They ran *that* fast? Damn," I'd think. I had a difficult time with one of the hardest lessons to learn in my sport: you can't dwell on the performance of others. When I was younger, I compensated by being much more brash than I am today.

Anson said I used to carry this look, like I was about to shut it down on everyone else. As though I just knew I was about to beat them. He wanted me to bring that energy back.

Anson has always been there for me throughout my career. I've leaned on him for advice and guidance ever since I emerged on the national scene. He was a great sprinter in his day. He competed in the Beijing Olympics but never reached the podium. Now he's a great mentor in the sport. He's the kind of guy who soaked up wisdom during his career and has a special way of sharing it. There is so much value in learning from the people who have been on the same journey as you. You can learn from their success and their mistakes. Often it's the people who have long careers, filled with ups and downs, who have the most to share. That's why I always turn to Anson when I need advice, even now. He's always on point. So when he speaks, I listen.

Anson admires guys like Donovan Bailey, who wore his confidence like a jersey. He carried a ferocity whenever he ran—a "this is *my* territory" sort of thing. Anson was trying to get me to bring back a bold era for Canadian sprinters.

As much as I respect Donovan, I am kind of the opposite.

I have confidence, but I didn't show it in the same way. Rather than being ferocious, I'm more of a smiler. But even though we were different, that didn't mean I had nothing to learn from the way guys like Donovan approached their races.

"Nothing personal" was Anson's way of nudging me back towards the edge I carried earlier on in my career.

"Just go out there, beat people, and don't take it personally," he told me.

This was one time, though, that I didn't take his advice.

"It's all good, man," I told Anson.

I understood what he meant and I appreciated it—as I do everything Anson tells me. I could see the potential benefit to approaching competition. But that kind of attitude was reflective of a younger, less experienced version of me. So I took the concept and flipped it around in a way I've found incredibly helpful.

To me "nothing personal" isn't so much about beating my opponents (or letting them know I intend to), but rather it's a reminder that my race isn't actually about the people I'm lined up against. I avoid being distracted by the noise of competition. I don't need to tell my opponents that I'm going to beat them. That's *why* I'm there; that's what we're all trying to do. Whether I win or not, personal conflict has nothing to do with it. It's about me being my best. That's the only thing that matters.

I want to win, and I'm going to do everything I can to leave everyone else behind me. I don't need to be cocky; I can let my performance speak for itself.

It took a while for me to realize it didn't matter how well my competitors were doing. I'd get caught up in the noise of results coming in from meets around the world. But I didn't factor in the nuance of a race—the varying weather conditions, wind speed and directions, the altitude, and even the track surface itself. Everything is just different.

That is one of the biggest lessons I've learned in my career. It's so hard to know if a competitor is actually faster than you. Just because they posted a better time doesn't necessarily mean they are that much faster than you. There are always many factors at play. You might be running at a meet where all the conditions are working against you—it's raining or it's cold—and you run a slower time. And then you *think* you're slower.

But later, you line up against that same person and you end up beating them. That's the only way you can actually measure yourself against a competitor. But even then, there are so many variables—nagging injuries, fatigue, spikes that just don't fit right. Their best doesn't necessarily mean they are better than you. You can line up against them thinking, "Wow, this person ran 9.8 and I've only run 10.0 this year." And then all of a sudden, you beat them. It's not that what they ran earlier is a fake time. It's just that it's a different time in different conditions in a different race.

The point is you can't control the variables. You can't control the unique factors that your opponents are dealing with, just as they can't control the issues that might slow you down. It's always possible to beat the person beside you, just as it's always possible that they will beat you.

I don't mean to say the competition itself isn't important. Of course it is. It's the entire reason you're there; it's everything.

But over the years I've learned I can't worry about what another person is running. I have no physical impact on what my competitors do.

Anson used to remind me when I got older that I still have plenty of time to prove myself.

"Don't worry about that guy," he'd tell me. "You'll beat him when the time is right."

Anson gave me confidence to believe that eventually my talent would prevail. But rather than focusing on my competitors, I needed to focus on beating the previous best version of me. That's really the only gauge that matters because it's the only one I have control over.

The best thing I could do was to focus on myself, getting better every day in practice by beating my previous times. That's exactly how you've got to approach progress. Every training session is a building block. Each time you run faster, it's like another step towards reaching the top.

If you're looking to improve, consider simplifying your goals in that way. Improve what you can each time you practise. Build on what you've already accomplished. Focus on those small improvements and you'll see the gains you're hoping for.

In competition, it's a little bit different. I still focus on achieving my best performance in the race. Through the years I've learned not to worry about the time on the clock. I just worry about winning when it matters. Along the way, I realized that when you start winning the race, the times will come.

When I won gold in the 200 metres at the Tokyo Olympics, I didn't aim to run 19.62 and break my national record. But I won—and the time came. It's kind of weird, because many of the guys I lined up with had run incredibly fast times all year, but I hadn't run at my best yet. Then the gun went off in Tokyo—and I set a new personal and Canadian record.

Success comes with exceeding expectations, not just meeting them. This is how I approach performing in the biggest moments. It's about setting a target and then beating it. I always try to aim beyond the target—and if I don't reach it, it's okay; there is still room for improvement. There's nothing wrong with falling short of your goals, whatever they might be, as frustrating as it is. Trust me, I have fallen short so many times in my life and my career. You can learn a lot in the process.

I came home from Tokyo with gold, silver, and bronze medals. Even though I didn't achieve my goal of triple gold, I still ended up with new personal best times in my individual events. I gave it my best effort. Now I'll continue to build off that.

My new target is 19.62. And my quest for three golds has moved to Paris.

There are still strides to take to make my ultimate dream happen. I use that as fuel and motivation to keep pushing through my career. I still have time to reach the targets I set in Tokyo. Because in competition that's the ultimate goal: to be better than your previous best.

18

CHEMISTRY

Sprinting is an isolating sport. On the surface, success or failure comes down to individual performance. You carry the glory of the victories, but you also carry the disappointment of defeat. Either way, it rests on your shoulders. Behind the scenes there are people—coaches, sports therapists, doctors, trainers, agents—who played an enormous role in those victories and share some responsibility in the defeats. But ultimately, it falls on the person who stands alone on the track.

That isolation doesn't bother me. I enjoy rising to the pressure it creates. But at the same time, I've always loved being part of a team. When I played competitive basketball and soccer, I was usually the team captain and I loved taking on the responsibility of that leadership role. I'm still a big basketball fan, and part of me envies the way elite basketball players must allow their talent to meld and flow with the talent of their teammates. A good basketball team holds a collective rhythm. The players are in sync in a way that allows them to function as a single unit, fundamental parts of a fine-tuned machine. That kind of connection develops a unique camaraderie among teammates. I love that.

I think my love for team sports is why I'm so drawn to the relay events in track. People are often surprised to learn I love running relays. But I think of it as a return to my roots in team sports. Through the relay specifically, I've learned a lot about the challenges and benefits of being part of a team in my career.

Being part of a team makes you better at the individual components of performance. You need to adapt and react to what your teammates are doing. You don't know what to expect. I love that dynamic. I love that camaraderie.

As a member of the national team, I've landed on the podium twice at the Olympics in the 4 x 100-metre relay. Through those experiences, I've learned that functioning within a team is a key part of finding success. We all have teammates—people working towards the same goals, with the same interests in mind. Knowing how to perform effectively with those teammates is key to achieving both your individual and collective goals.

As with most team sports, a lot more goes into a performance than what a spectator might see from the sidelines or watch from home.

I think the relay is the toughest event I compete in because it's unpredictable. You can't control anything happening around you. The position you and your teammates find themselves in depends on the performance of everyone else. When I run the final leg, I watch as the first leg passes to the second leg, and the second passes to the third leg, getting closer and closer to me. I rely on my teammates to get me the baton. They rely on me to take it and either come from behind or keep a lead. Either way, all the work they have put into the race transfers to me. It's my responsibility. We all play a critical role in the process, and if one of us doesn't bring our best that day, we all lose. That's what happened to me during that first national team event in Glasgow when I was just starting to compete on the international stage and felt overwhelmed. My mistake in the exchange cost me and all three of my teammates a chance at the podium. It caused me a ton of embarrassment and self-loathing, until my more experienced teammates taught me the real value of competing with a group. Through their support and empathy, they showed me that even in a sport that focuses on individual accomplishment, you can lean on quality teammates.

Living in the Olympic Village creates a unique opportunity to connect with my teammates. In Tokyo, I was running with Jerome Blake, Brendon Rodney, and Aaron Brown. Of course, I'd known all these guys through the national team and competition. Aaron and I were competitors in the 100 and 200 metres, but we were also teammates. When it came to the relay, we had one unified goal and were excited about achieving it together. We were in a great position, with no clear favourite in the field. Three of us had won bronze in Rio and were ready to reach the podium again. Over the course of the Rio Games, I think we all got to know each other a lot more on a personal level. We developed a special bond. I think you need to develop that kind of relationship with one another to succeed.

It started before we even got to the village. We all know each other; we all talk to each other often—so we already had a connection. We'd just laugh and have fun together. We related to each other as people, not just as sprinters. That continued when we arrived in Tokyo. We connected in very simple ways to pass the time, probably the ways most teammates do. We played dominoes and cards against each other, we watched shows, we sat around talking, kind of the way you would with a university roommate. So we knew each other on a personal level, which I think is helpful in establishing the kind of trust and familiarity it takes to reach peak performance as a group.

One of the unique components of our group was that we shared leadership responsibilities. We valued each other's opinions, and each had a voice in how we'd approach our race. We came together as a team and asked: What do we want to accomplish here? What are our goals? Do we want a personal best? Do we want to win an Olympic medal? Do we want to win a gold medal?

This was an actual conversation we had. Obviously everyone wants to win and will say so—but this was an honest talk between teammates about what was realistic and how we felt about that. We wanted to establish what we believed was possible and what outcome we'd all be proud to leave Tokyo with. In my experience working in a team, I think this is a valuable approach to ensuring that everyone is on the same path with the same goals in mind. Clarify what your collective goals are, and make sure they are aligned before you set out to achieve them.

We decided we wanted to be the best. We wanted to make our families proud. We wanted to make Canada proud. If we did everything we could towards achieving those goals, we'd be happy with our effort.

A lot of preparation goes into competing as a relay team. We had several meetings, where we would talk to each other ahead of competition. We'd spend an hour together watching films of races to see what we could work on in training. We'd study the transition from the first leg to the second leg, figuring out just how many steps we were taking to the person ahead. It had to be exact, as I found out the hard way all those years ago at the Commonwealth Games in 2014, watching Bolt and everyone else cross the finish line while I stood on the track having missed our exchange.

You need to have a connection with your teammates to know they're not going to leave too soon or wait too long. If you're going to get out of that exchange zone, you need to have built a bond with each other. When you have that kind of confidence in your teammates, it creates an essential trust. You have faith that the guys beside you have put in the same amount of work and are aligned with the same vision. Without that kind of reliance, I think you are unlikely to succeed as a group.

In the end, our connection on both a personal and professional level—from playing dominoes to studying film together—strengthened the chemistry between us. That's what it's all about. We did everything collectively as a team, and that's what brings out the best in one another.

I think that's what makes running relays so fun for me, because I love teaming up with the guys. You miss out on that in an individual sport like sprinting. There is a difference between the thrill of chasing greatness alone and what it's like to chase victory as part of the group. I just love going from my individual events in the 100 and 200 metres to finishing things off with a relay. In solo events you miss the connection of teammates sometimes, that feeling that together you can achieve something special.

I would tell the team all the time: We are *this* close. We *can* win a gold medal. It's wide open, there's no favourite. We have a chance to actually come home with a medal here. And we can break the national record. After I won gold in the 200, I think that as a group we started to believe we could do something special in the relay. If I could do it, there was no reason we all couldn't do it together.

Aaron put us in a great position off the start alongside Britain and Japan as the front-runner. He passed the baton to Jerome, who held us in medal contention down the backstretch. Japan missed their exchange, which took them out of the race. Brendon battled China's Su Bingtian, Britain's Richard Kilty, and Jamaica's Yohan Blake on the bend to keep us in medal contention. China bobbled their hand-off, slowing them down. We were a few metres behind when Brendon passed the baton to me. It was a perfect exchange, allowing me to explode into the final stretch. I took off, trying to catch Italy's Filippo Tortu and Great Britain's Nethaneel Mitchell-Blake. I crossed the line third, securing another podium finish, with a time of 37.70.

We were all happy with the outcome, knowing we'd finished with a time no Canadians had accomplished before. I think we are all proud of each other and happy with our success. We were grateful. There was a relief that we medalled because we knew we had a shot to get on the podium—but we were aiming for gold. We were happy with bronze, but we weren't satisfied. Months later, Great Britain would be disqualified for a failed drug test, bumping us up to silver from bronze.

But still, our ultimate focus as a team was gold. We knew we were going to get better as a unit. Every year we've improved. As a team, we agreed we would continue to evolve and focus on our goals. And when the time came, we'd team up again and make it happen.

It's just a reality of life that you can do your best and fall a bit short. In our case, we did our best, but it still wasn't enough to land us on top of the podium. So when we arrived in Oregon for the World Championships the following summer, we were determined to be even better.

But the opportunity came at a time when I was at my worst. Coming off the Olympic year, which was pushed to 2021 because of the COVID pandemic, I struggled to get back to my peak level of performance. I suffered a foot injury during training that kept me from accelerating out of the blocks the way I'd worked so hard to improve. Then in June, while competing in the Diamond League in Europe, I caught COVID for a second time, after having it early that winter. It sidelined me for weeks and the effects lingered long after.

Many people speculated I might skip the World Championships altogether because of my health, but I wasn't going to miss an opportunity to compete on one of the sport's biggest stages.

It was a frustrating start. I just didn't have the energy to compete the way I needed to. After I was unable to make the finals in the 100-metre race, I made the difficult decision to drop out of the 200, knowing I just wasn't at my best.

But I was already scheduled to run anchor on the 4 x 100 team, and I didn't want to let my teammates down—or return home empty-handed. We had something to prove at the 2022 World Championships, having won bronze in 2015 but failing to reach the podium at the last worlds in Doha in 2019. All four members of the silver-winning team from Tokyo were back. So we were confident we could do something special, even though we weren't favoured to even reach the podium. The fact that everyone viewed us as an underdog team only made us more determined to prove everyone wrong.

There were Canadian flags everywhere inside Hayward Field, the track and field centre at the University of Oregon's campus. It was such a contrast to competing in Tokyo, where no fans had been allowed. Seeing people dressed in red and white, and the maple leaf flags waving throughout the stands, gave me chills.

I lined up beside Marvin Bracy, who was running anchor for the heavily favoured Americans. Bracy had just won silver in the 100 metres. But Aaron, Jerome, Brendon, and I weren't interested in what the doubters had to say. We wanted to continue what we'd started in Tokyo. We were determined to run faster than we ever had before. Once again, we laid out our goals before competing. We watched video of past races and identified our weak spots. We had a game plan. By pulling myself out of the 200 metres, I had more time to rest and prepare for the relay. We were able to get in more reps as a team and make sure we were in sync.

When the gun sounded at Hayward Field, we were ready. I watched my teammates in each leg of the race, ripping down the track, doing exactly what we needed, each passing the baton to the next—trusting that we'd each do our part to bring it home. Brendon passed the responsibility to me, and I took off down the final stretch. I heard the roar of Canadian fans in the crowd when I crossed the line just ahead of Bracy.

We'd won. I let out a triumphant shout as my legs slowed and my teammates rushed to celebrate.

We'd done it: gold. The fastest team in the world. Our time of 37.48 broke our own national record.

Everyone seemed to be shocked but us. We knew we'd put in the work as a team and that even though we weren't at our best heading into the final, we had the preparation, chemistry, and trust in each other to beat the best version of ourselves.

Collectively, we'd pushed for new goals, always looking for a way to be that much better. In Tokyo we succeeded but came up short of the prize we wanted. In Oregon, we returned determined to accomplish more. We had to be a great team to be able to pull that off.

On a personal level, I wasn't at my best—I wasn't able to accomplish my individual goals. In a frustrating year, I was grateful to find success alongside my teammates.

That's the best thing about being part of a good team. You support each other and push each other forward, somehow getting the best out of each other when you can't seem to do it on your own.

You become one body, racing towards the same goal.

19

QUESTION MARKS

This might be it for me.

The thought haunted me after I was blindsided by a hamstring injury for the first time. Everything in life was going well. And then all of a sudden it crashed.

I was in the best shape of my life heading into the World Championships in London, in August 2017. My life had changed a year earlier when I won three medals at the Rio Olympics. I was well known in the track world before standing on that podium, but the Olympics are the biggest stage in sport and suddenly it seemed like everyone knew who I was. The media had loved to play up the friendly rivalry between me and Usain Bolt in Rio. Now he was in the last stage of his career and had said the World Championships would be his final event. I was running as well as ever and wanted to face Bolt in the 100-metre final. It was my last chance to beat the greatest of all time. I knew I could catch him. The entire year, that race had been my focus.

A few days before the World Championships were set to open, I ran through a practice session at Mile End Stadium in London. We were focusing on my starts, making sure I could explode enough out of the blocks to hang in with the other runners through the first 20 metres. During one of the practice runs, I took off and immediately felt a snap in the back of my right leg.

It was my hamstring. At first I thought it was just a cramp and figured it would be fine by the time I woke up the next morning. But when I woke up, the adrenalin was no longer pumping and I was in serious pain, barely able to move my leg. I flew to Munich to see a specialist through Puma in hopes they might somehow find a way for me to still be able to compete. But there wasn't. The doctor told me it was a grade 2 tear—and recommended I miss the World Championships. That meant stepping aside while others ran the 100, 200, and 4 x 100-metre relay in the biggest event of the year.

"To not have this opportunity is unimaginable to me but it is the reality I am faced with," I wrote in a statement announcing the news. "I am sad to miss this chance, but I am young and will be back and better than ever in the near future."

On the surface I played it cool. My coach, Stu McMillan, noted how chill I was but expected it would sink in while I watched the races go on without me.

Really, I was devastated. I've always been good at shielding my emotions. I'm able to stay relaxed on the outside, even when I'm down. Injuries are a part of sport, so I knew this could happen. But I was still as frustrated as I'd ever been in my career.

To get injured three days before one of my biggest races ever, outside the Olympics—I couldn't believe it. At that stage in my career, I was still trying to make a name for myself. I was still trying to win my first gold medal on a big stage.

"Is this real?" I thought. "Did this actually just happen? My hamstring just gave out on me *now*?"

The disappointment I felt then would soon get much worse.

At first, we thought I'd miss only five to six weeks to rest and rehab my hamstring. That meant I'd miss the Diamond League final at the start of September. I was ranked first in the 100 and second in the 200 on the circuit at the time, so it was frustrating—but I could live with it.

I didn't realize what lay ahead.

Looking back now, I know I wasn't prepared for the mental valley. I'd just come off one of my greatest years ever, winning three medals at my first Olympics—and now I was out with an injury that can derail a sprinter's career. The hamstring injury was the toughest thing I'd had to overcome to that point in my career. I guess it's fair to say I hadn't been in the sport that long at the time—I know there are likely more challenges ahead. But this was the first significant injury I'd suffered in any sport. It was the first time I'd been physically incapable of doing what I usually did.

As I went through the rehab process that winter, everything felt slow. I'd do a workout feeling like a force was holding me back. I'd think, "Man, I used to kill this workout."

When I was able to get back on the track, I'd do practice runs but couldn't perform. It was disappointment after disappointment. I could feel the doubt hanging over me.

"Am I really not going to be the same guy?" I wondered.

Everyone kept telling me to be patient. It was a process. Rome wasn't built in a day, right? I knew all that, but patience in practice is much more difficult than patience in theory. I constantly had to remind myself that this was going to take time. I had to trust in that.

But it was incredibly tough. I hadn't faced adversity like that before.

At times I wanted to give up. I wanted to be done. It felt like I'd stumbled my way into an opportunity I didn't deserve. I'd somehow managed to trick everyone into believing I was fast. I'd somehow managed to win three Olympic medals. But all this time, I was a fraud. It was as if I just wanted to take the money and run, as they say—to leave before everyone realized I never actually belonged to begin with. I remember feeling like I'd let down so many people who believed in me.

I know it sounds crazy, but those are the kinds of thoughts I battled with. There were times when I thought, "Damn, this might be it for me."

Now I realize that this happens to everybody. We're often harder on ourselves than we need to be. It doesn't necessarily matter what profession you're in. It's a part of life. We want to make the people we love proud of who we are. And when your self-worth is tied up in accomplishments, it creates the illusion that those accomplishments are the only reason you matter. So when those accomplishments don't come—when you just can't run anymore—you're left feeling like you've failed.

It was hard for me to see my peers and everyone around me excel, while I felt stuck in the same spot.

My hamstring didn't heal as quickly as we'd hoped, and I just didn't feel right when the season opened up again in the spring of 2018. It didn't help that I'd caught mono that winter and the effects lingered for months, setting my training back even further. But I pushed obvious concerns aside because I wanted to be back on the track so badly. I ignored the apprehension I was feeling, dismissing it as a mental block—a subconscious fear that I would reinjure my hamstring.

I should have listened to my gut.

After sitting out the Commonwealth Games in April, I'd had a difficult start to the 2018 season. I ran 20.26 in the 200 at the Diamond League season-opening meet in Doha in early May. A week later, I finished last in the 100 in 10.25 at a Diamond League meet in Shanghai. I took six weeks off after that meet to recuperate—and deal with some more pressing business.

At the same time that I was enduring turmoil and doubt in my career on the track, my life took on a whole new meaning when my girlfriend Nia gave birth to our daughter, Yuri. It was an incredible, life-changing moment. Suddenly, I was a dad—and nothing I could do on the track would ever be more important than that.

But it also meant I had a whole new responsibility. I had to provide for our daughter, for my family—I had to make sure we had everything we needed in this life. I felt that pressure. There was only a short window in which I could earn a living that would provide my family with a life I couldn't have imagined when I was younger. That meant I needed to get back on the track; I couldn't let these opportunities pass.

In July, I looked to defend my national title in the 100 and 200 metres at the Canadian Track and Field Championships in Ottawa.

It had been eleven long months since I'd sustained the injury in London, and I was finally starting to feel like myself on the track. I wasn't entirely there yet, but I was closer than I'd been in nearly a year—so I decided the nationals were the perfect place to put an exclamation point on my return.

But all I added was a question mark.

Instead of defending my title, I struggled to make the 100-metre final. And in the final, I slipped to third, running 10.21, while Aaron Brown finished first. It was as fast and hard as I had run in a while, but I knew then that I still wasn't myself. I'd put a pretty big load on my body in the race, considering my time away, but I felt like I could handle it.

I stuck it out hoping for a better result in the 200. It was my first time doubling up with both races in a meet since I'd been injured. Ahead of the semifinals I felt better and thought I had a good chance to repeat as champion and finally put this injury behind me.

During my semifinal heat at Terry Fox Stadium, I carried the lead around the bend and into the straightaway. But with 50 metres to go I felt a sharp cramp in my right hamstring.

I pulled up.

Damn.

I knew it.

I walked across the finish line as all those feelings of disappointment and doubt flooded back. I waved to the fans, who kindly stood and clapped for me, knowing what I'd been through.

I was so frustrated. I was beaten. But I wore a brave face for the media afterwards.

"It's part of the game. You win some, you lose some," I told a writer from the Canadian Press. "And you've just got to take your losses and come back strong and try to make the best of it."

Usually, I believe that. But despite my chill exterior, I was more disappointed than I'd been at any point since injuring my hamstring for the first time the previous summer.

An MRI revealed I'd suffered a grade 1 strain of my biceps femoris, one of the hamstring muscles in the same leg I'd injured before.

I was down on myself right away. It was a bad decision to compete at the nationals at all—I'd known it in my gut. I should have known better. I should have listened to how my body felt. I should have taken more time and focused more on rehab. I knew I wasn't ready.

Not knowing what would happen next was nerve-racking. I didn't know the next steps. I knew stories about athletes who suffered hamstring injuries that basically ended their careers. They never returned to what they were before. It was over—they were never the same again. That thought was always in the back of my mind. I was filled with anxiety, questioning whether I was going to make it back.

"Am I ever going to be the same athlete again? Would I be the same person who shocked the world by winning three medals at my first Olympics?" I wondered. "Would I ever be *me* again?"

When I suffered that second hamstring injury, I was even more worried that this was it for me. I remember thinking, "This must be it. I can't get back to where I was before." It was crazy.

At that point, I was nearly defeated. It was the darkest place I'd ever been.

Everybody reaches moments in life that seem impossible to get through. For an athlete, an injury that can end your career is devastating. But even if you're not an athlete, you know that sinking feeling that everything in your life is about to fall apart.

You feel like the pain you're going through is more than you can handle. You feel like the loss you've endured is too great. Maybe life just feels heavy, and you're not quite sure why.

Often, just when it seems like you've overcome an enormous challenge, you're blindsided by another one. It can seem more crushing than the first.

But that doesn't mean you can just give up. You've got to find hope. You've got to believe there is a purpose for what you're going through—that it's all part of your journey to where you're supposed to be.

Before that year, between 2017 and 2018, I don't think I actually knew much about adversity. When I look back, I can see that it built a lot of character in me.

I learned how to keep pushing despite the doubt, and to believe things are going to work out. It also ended up being one of the formative periods of my life.

But it wasn't easy. These things never are. I still had a long way to go before I'd fully understand that.

At the time, I felt like everything was out of my control.

Despite all the work I put into rehabilitating my hamstring, it was still susceptible to reinjury. That meant my entire career, my ability to earn for my family, was at risk too. I'd always been confident, but now I was having serious doubts. It was a humbling journey. A lot of people thought my career was over, that I'd never be the same. I'd been a star attraction at track meets around the world, but now promoters wouldn't even give me a lane.

It seemed like everything I had worked to build in my life was on the verge of being taken away. Suddenly all the success I'd enjoyed—the podium finishes, the cheering fans, the sponsorship deals—was disappearing.

But as a pro athlete, I know this wasn't unique. And I know most people can relate to finding themselves in a situation where nothing feels certain. It's shocking how quickly it can happen. It can be a job loss, a serious injury, an illness, the death of a loved one, a broken relationship—or any other unexpected turn that reveals just how vulnerable you were all along. It's a terrifying place to be.

But it's in those moments that you realize just how much you truly have. I was surrounded by family who supported and inspired me throughout my darkest days. And I was blessed to have experts to lean on for guidance and strength. Still, there were times amid it all where I felt hopeless. I can only imagine what some people feel facing much more challenging circumstances. But if you look around you, I think you're likely to find that you're surrounded by love and support too—even if it seems hard to find. When everything else is gone, we're left with what matters. What is that for you? And who? Find hope and strength in those answers.

20

MAKE TOUGH CHOICES

C hange is good. It's necessary. But it's something a lot of people are afraid of. I've seen that so many times with different athletes throughout the years. I know competitors who stick with the same system—same coach, same trainers—year after year. They're afraid to do anything out of the ordinary.

Comfort can be a barrier to success if you're not careful.

In early 2016, after I'd made the difficult decision to move on from college and go pro, I faced a lot of criticism. Some people felt I had sold out. They felt I hadn't been loyal to USC and skipped out the moment I had an opportunity to cash in.

But I had to ignore the critics. I knew I had made the right decision for me. I was happy about it, and I believed in what I was doing. I think that's what it comes down to in the end. As long as you're happy about your decision and you're not having second thoughts or regrets, things will work out.

That's always been an approach that has worked for me. I try to give that same advice to other athletes who are in the same position, at a crossroads unsure of what to do. I tell them to do their homework and to listen to advice from people they trust. Weigh the pros and cons of the situation.

But ultimately, I tell them to trust their gut instinct. Don't second-guess what you feel. Don't discredit your own intuition. Have confidence in it. No one knows you better than you do.

You need to be in charge of the decisions you're making in your life. For me, as a track athlete, there is even more pressure to look out for myself. That's also why being discerning about who is in your inner circle is so crucial.

The best people to listen to are the ones who have nothing to gain from your decision. Their advice is just advice, without personal motive. I've met people I decided I couldn't listen to, because it was clear they had something to gain from the outcome of my decision.

I've always had confidence in my intuition. It's something that is just part of my personality. I'm very laid back, but I pay attention. I observe what people around me are doing. I give people chances to prove themselves—and if I have doubts, I give them the chance to prove me wrong. I don't make decisions hastily. I'm good at being patient and thinking these things through. I have confidence in that process.

Maybe that's a skill I've had for a long time. Maybe I observed it growing up, through the way my mother made decisions about our life. I'm certain she taught me a few tricks when I was younger. I am always aware of who is with me and who isn't. When someone is just genuinely interested in helping you navigate a decision, those are the kinds of people you should seek guidance from.

Even back in high school, I made the decision to switch schools because I wanted a school with better athletic programming. As a kid, a lot of people told me I was being inconsistent, jumping around and being indecisive. They told me I was being irrational. But really, I was just being thoughtful and purposeful in the decisions I was making.

//////

I've switched coaches several times in my career so far, although the first few changes were early in my career when I was just starting and in college.

After Tony took a chance on me, I moved on to learn from Coach Wood at Coffeyville—and from there was recruited by Coach Caryl and Coach Watts at USC.

Each of them played an important role in my development as a sprinter. Each of them is still part of my life today—the coaching foundation of my success.

In the spring of 2016, I moved to Arizona to train at ALTIS—formerly known as the World Athletics Center—working with renowned coach Stu McMillan. I was impressed by the plan that Stu and coach Kevin Tyler laid out for me when I first met with them. They had a vision to take me to the next level. My approach to weightlifting, in particular, had been lax. They felt I could add speed with a more targeted approach to gaining power in the gym.

My move to Coach Stu was different from those previous changes. He was the first coach I actively hired to guide my development as a pro athlete. That decision marked a significant moment in my growth as a sprinter.

I rented an apartment near Scottsdale about 15 minutes from

the track at Paradise Valley Community College, where we trained.

As the months went on in my new home, I felt my strength building. I could see the improvement. I was getting faster.

Stu understood that I was juggling many commitments having just turned pro—and he was willing to work around my schedule. Not a lot of coaches understand those pressures on an athlete or are able to accommodate them. He told me to not stress about it— to do what I had to do and then we'd get back to work. I was so new to everything that his reassurance helped me ease into the new realities of my life. I appreciated that so much. I was like a sponge listening to him. I tried to soak in all of his knowledge, while figuring out what worked for me and what didn't.

After Rio, I knew I'd been right to block out all the criticism about turning pro. But since then, I've switched coaches twice. That's not very common in track.

I've found success, so far, with each of my previous coaches. Before my most recent switch in the fall of 2022, I've medalled with every single coach I've had.

For me it's not always about the coach, specifically. I've had a good relationship with each coach and have learned more about myself and my ability from each of them. Each of my coaches has helped me improve in different ways.

To find success, you need to be aware of what is working and what isn't—be willing to make the necessary changes to get where you want to be.

I've had to make many tough decisions in my career, moving on from coaches or trainers, to make sure I'm not plateauing. As difficult as those moments are, I've always been good at knowing when things have run their course.

In an individual sport, like sprinting, an athlete needs to make critical decisions about the team around them. In other team sports, a front office makes those calls. Executives make calls about coaches, trainers, and the support systems around their players. But as a track athlete, you are the president and general manager of your own career. You're in charge of everything. You hire agents to help make key decisions, you hire coaches to help reach peak performance, and you hire trainers and specialists, like masseuses and chiropractors, to help repair and rebuild your body. All of those decisions fall to you, and that's a lot of pressure.

Over the course of my career, I've learned the importance of being able to make difficult decisions and to make changes when needed. It's always tough, because regardless of the advice I get from the support group I've built around me, at the end of the day, it's my decision.

If I decide to hire a trainer or a coach—or if I decide to move on from one—I'm on my own in that. It's what makes my kind of career so complicated.

I have so many people in my ear telling me to do this, or to do that—or not to do this, or not to do that. I value their opinions. They are in my inner circle for a reason. All of those people mean well, but they can't see everything from my perspective. No one else can walk in my shoes. Not being able to see the entire picture, they can be completely wrong. At the end of the day, I'm the one who has to live with the decisions I make, not them.

I've learned that I need to do my own homework and not rely on others to do it for me. Because at some point, I will have to make the call. I can't worry about what everybody else has to say.

I pride myself on being able to take in information from various people I trust, and then making my own decision. Leaders need to be able to block out the noise and trust themselves—and I think of myself as the CEO of my destiny. In the end, I carry the responsibility for the outcomes of my career. I have to make the tough choices about who I work with and when I decide to move on from those relationships. I need to decide whether the advice I'm given is worth taking. It's a lot to take on, but at this level, I have to be confident in my ability to make those decisions.

That is a key component to personal success.

When you face a big decision, don't rush. Do your research ahead of time, and seek guidance from people you trust and who have the experience to see what you might be missing. But be comfortable with making tough calls. Ignore the noise. Block out all the negativity. If someone is not supporting you, then that's not somebody you want to be around.

And once you've done your homework, make your own call.

///////

When you make the difficult decision to leave behind something that has worked for you in the past, don't think of it as though you're just picking up and leaving.

People always say that when you start something, you've got to finish it. And I believe that. But I don't think it's the same situation as making changes to better suit your goals. My primary objective as an athlete is to do what's best for me.

If something is no longer working in your pursuit of your goals, then why should you stick with it?

People often say you should wait it out and see if things change. In certain situations that works. If it's too late to pull out, then I agree—go and finish it. But what I'm saying is, if you're not happy with something, then why continue to do it? What ultimate purpose does that serve?

Do what you think is right and ignore the outside noise, especially after you've made a decision. There will be negatives to the decision you've made. There always are. Hopefully, in the end there are more pros than cons. But don't dwell on the balance between the negative and the positive. Don't second-guess. Lean into your decision and give yourself the best opportunity possible to succeed.

My decision to move to Phoenix to work with Stu McMillan at ALTIS paid off. The shift in my training took me to the next level.

I returned from the Rio Olympics with three medals—and I had forced the world to take notice of me.

Two years later, after battling through two hamstring injuries, I decided to move on from my time with Stu. Frustrated by the injuries, I knew it was just time to try something new. You get a feel for when things aren't working anymore. It's up to the coach to adjust that. Sometimes you reach a point where it feels like they've used up all their secrets, all their techniques—and they don't know what else to do to get you to the next level. At that point, you should consider a new methodology. Sometimes a switch to a new coach helps push you to a new level, building on what your previous coaches helped you achieve.

But even though I no longer work directly with Stu, I'm still in regular contact with him today. I ask for his advice and guidance because I value it. When we parted ways, the change was much more about my needing something new—after so much frustration with my injuries—than about any sort of animosity. In fact, looking back, I can see that I became a bit too lax in my training after the Rio Olympics. Completing my education took me away from a rigorous system, and my commitments off the track consumed a lot of my time. I was still learning to balance the demands of life as a pro—and I think it might have left me vulnerable to injury the following summer. In hindsight, I can see that. But I can also see that my decision to move on was what I needed, and it worked for me.

/////

In track, moving to a new coach requires much more than working with a new person. For me, it usually means I'm uprooting my family.

Coaches are typically set up in a location where they have access to a track and a weight room. It's very hard for them to move around and go somewhere else and find a new facility. So most of the time you have to go to them.

It works better from a financial standpoint. They usually have their own set-up with a training centre from which they rent time on the track and in the weight room, which costs a certain amount each month. Often they have a relationship with a physiotherapist as well. The coach uses the money we pay them to pay for the facility and other costs on top of their income. It's kind of like a one-stop shop.

A coach is usually in the same place for years. The reality is that quality tracks are hard to find. There aren't many facilities that operate privately or specifically for professional use. The sport remains somewhat amateur in that way. Usually only a university has the kind of money to build a quality set-up, so you're competing with varsity programs for use of the facility. We end up having to work around those schedules, which adds another complicating layer to training.

When you are working out as a member of the national team it's a bit easier. There are several indoor and outdoor centres in Toronto where I can access time to train privately, including York University and the Toronto Pan Am Sports Centre. It's a great set-up for Canadian athletes, which I'm very appreciative to have access to. But when you're living in another country, it's a different story. They might have that set-up for American athletes, but not for foreigners.

Most of the top sprint coaches live outside of Canada, so I have to go abroad to work with them. It's also better for your body to train in a warmer climate, instead of spending half the year on the tight turns of an indoor track, which are hard on ankles, knees, and other joints.

It's always a time-consuming process. These are big decisions that will shape your approach to the biggest races of your career. You go through an interview process, narrowing down options. Then you figure out logistics—whether you can make this kind of transition work, not only from a training perspective but from a life perspective as well.

Nia and I needed to find a coach who could train both the hurdles and sprints, which was challenging. It gets expensive to rent out a track for three or four hours every single day. Coaches need to work with several athletes to make it work for them. Often, shoe companies will hire a coach to work with the athletes signed to their brand. So you will have a group of Nike athletes working together, an Adidas group, and a Puma group. It gives athletes more options for where they can go to get the best available coaching.

In the end, that was how Nia and I managed to work with renowned track coach Rana Reider, who had been coaching in the Netherlands but decided to make the move to Jacksonville, Florida.

Even if you don't have to make a huge geographical move when you decide to make a change in your life, those decisions often disrupt the comfort and flow of our lives. A big decision breaks our routines. But when a routine isn't working, you need to be bold enough to make a move so you don't get stuck in the pursuit of your goals. Discomfort is growth, sometimes. Don't let your fear of it allow your potential to stagnate.

///////

In the fall of 2018, I packed up my life in Phoenix and moved to Jacksonville, Florida, to train with Rana. Again, the change worked out. Working with Rana, I found my way back into peak form—despite all the setbacks the pandemic brought. I believe that decision played an important role in preparing me for Tokyo, where I added three more Olympic medals—including the gold I'd been seeking for so long.

But the following season, I battled a foot injury that plagued me in 2022. Aside from winning gold at the World Championships in the 4 x 100-metre relay alongside Aaron Brown, Jerome Blake, and Brendon Rodney, it was a frustrating year. After achieving my Olympic dream, I faced so many setbacks. I started to feel as though I wasn't reaching my potential.

Dealing with that nagging injury. Dealing with COVID—twice. Despite my training, I couldn't reclaim my speed. I'd rest but still feel exhausted. I just couldn't get back to where I needed to be.

And that's the name of the game. You have to stay healthy and stay fit. The hard part is always trying to figure out how to do that.

That summer, I found myself contemplating big decisions. What went wrong? What changes did I need to make? Did I need a new coach? Did I need to train differently? What could I have done better? That's what I was left trying to learn as I geared up for the next stage.

All of a sudden, the next Olympics in 2024 didn't seem very far away. I was already at the point where I had to decide what direction I was taking, in order to be at the peak of my ability when I arrived in Paris. The decision had to come now.

It was time to move on from my partnership with Rana. We had some successful years and then we had a down year. And so that was it. As hard as it can be to make a big move, the decision should be as simple as that.

At the end of the season, I travelled to Orlando to meet with some potential new coaches. It was like starting all over again. But Nia and I knew it was the right time to make the transition. We decided to make Orlando home.

The move meant we had to find a new house and settle our kids into a new school. It was nerve-racking.

But it was the right decision for us.

In whatever you pursue, be confident in your ability to make tough choices. Don't be afraid to make the changes required to take you to the next level of what you seek to achieve. It's not always easy, but it's necessary. Action is almost always better than inaction, especially when your progress is stagnating.

It's about recognizing when you are reaching that point. There is a moment when you realize the system you've set in place around you just can't take you any further. It can be a mental thing or a physical thing. Sometimes it might be the coach. They might just not know what to do next. Or it could just be that you need a new approach to shake things up, the way a basketball team sometimes needs a new coach, even though the current coach is clearly good at their job. Whatever the issue, you need to be willing and ready to adjust—to find another way.

I've reached moments in my career where it seemed like I'd reached my peak. But I've always refused to accept that.

I'm young. I'm not close to my peak yet. But in those moments, with the coach I had and the approach we were taking to training, I'd reached a temporary plateau. The way I view it, I needed to make a decision about that process if I wanted to keep rising. I needed to make a change so I could keep improving.

I put a lot of my confidence in my coach, and if that erodes, I have to be honest about it. It's a feeling. It's not that anything drastic has changed in our approach. As an athlete, I want to show constant improvement, and when I'm not progressing, I need to understand why.

Sometimes you just have to switch coaches to unlock something. I've witnessed that with competitors like Trayvon Bromell and Fred Kerley, a couple of the fastest men in the world. Trayvon worked and worked but kept getting frustrating results. Then he finally made a switch to a new coach—the same one I was working with—and he hit a new level of success. Fred made a change as well and won gold in the 100 metres at the 2022 World Championships.

Sometimes it's not just the athlete, but a combination of the environment and the coaches around the athlete and the resources they can provide.

Sometimes it's very hard for a coach to multi-task and be able to give each individual the attention and focus they need. It's easy for a coach to get overwhelmed. That's what separates the good coaches from the not-so-good coaches. A good coach is able to say: "I can get *this* person to run fast, and I can get *this* person to run fast—and I can get *this* person to run fast." It's not just a one-size-fits-all approach.

There are situations where pride comes into play. A coach will dig in their heels and say: "No, this works. It's my way. You just have to get with the program."

Sometimes that works. Sometimes it doesn't.

Each coach has a different philosophy. A good coach will study an athlete to find out what's working for them—and what they need to be working on. What works for one athlete might not work for another. You have to see their strengths and their weaknesses—and be able to adapt, adjust, and make changes, depending on the athlete. Some coaches can't do that. Whether it's pride or stubbornness, they don't change their approach.

That's why it's so critical to be humble and willing to learn from anyone with experience who can help you grow. Even if you don't necessarily agree with them on everything, being open to new ideas and approaches will help you better understand what does and doesn't work for you. It doesn't matter if you're an athlete, an entrepreneur, a student, or pursuing something else that requires constant growth. Effective growth comes from being in a state of constant learning.

But along with being open and willing to learn, it's critical to know when the value in those kinds of relationships begins to stagnate. Sometimes someone can help you for a couple of years, but then they don't know exactly what to do after that. In my case, that might mean moving on from a coach, physical therapist, or agent. But maybe it's a mentor, or a business partner. It might mean cutting back on certain relationships with friends who are no longer benefiting you. It can be hard to step away from people you're comfortable with if they are becoming a hindrance to your goals, but it needs to happen.

Because growth requires change. You can't think that what you did last year is going to make you an Olympic or world champion again. You need to keep focusing on new things—on what can work to get you even faster, because the person behind you is racing to catch up.

Maybe you ran 9.90 last year to win. Well, this year that 9.90 isn't going to be good enough to win. Now you have to be able to run 9.85, because everyone else is getting faster.

It's so easy to be complacent. It happens a lot. Athletes and coaches can both get too comfortable, especially when they've enjoyed previous success together.

I've noticed that a lot. I've noticed it in myself.

After reaching the podium at the Rio Olympics, I think I got complacent and felt like I could just easily get there again. I won a silver medal in the 200 metres in Rio with 20.02. But that time wasn't going to win a silver medal at the next Olympics. To win a gold medal in Tokyo I had to run under 20 seconds: 19.62. In fact, the top five in that race all ran it in under 20 seconds.

After you achieve success, you've got to keep going. You can't take your foot off the gas—because there is a constant drive to go faster.

You have to figure out how to push yourself that much further, to run that much quicker. Because eventually people catch up. They are learning about themselves, figuring out their mistakes and what they could have done better. They are embracing new technology, faster spikes, or improving their training and recovery systems. There are so many different ways for people to improve. I've seen it so many times where someone struggled the year before and all of a sudden will be on fire the next year. They just figured out things that work for them.

And that's really what this sport is about: finding ways to get better by milliseconds. That's what success in any field is about too: working to get better incrementally. Finding any fair advantage you can.

You can fix this one little thing and realize, "Oh, that's the difference right there." Because it's no longer the big things. Not when you reach a certain level. It's all the small things that make a difference.

People always seem shocked when someone who isn't a front-runner shows up vastly improved from the season before. That person might not have been a contender in the past, but they were capable. And now they're eating better, getting more sleep. They're less stressed. And then of course, on the track, a coach might have seen something they didn't see before. Now that runner is coming out of the blocks more explosively than before. Or they worked on their core in the off-season and are running upright and with more power.

It's those small things that help you figure out what's happening in your performance.

Make changes to help you achieve those small improvements.

That might mean changing who you work with. It might mean changing how you work. It might be something big, or it might be something small. But be aware of what you need to adjust as you strive to reach your goals. Because without deliberate change, you're likely to stay exactly where you are.

21

FAITH AND ACTION

I wear a cross on a chain around my neck when I race. It's a symbol of the faith that has carried me through adversity in my life. That's how my mom raised me. I grew up Catholic, but when I was a bit older, we started going to a non-denominational church for a while. When you are surrounded by faith, it becomes part of who you are. My mom is still a staunch Catholic.

I won't claim to be the most devout Christian today, but faith has always been a significant part of my life. I'll always be the boy my mom raised in that way.

I should practise it much more than I do. But I still try to stay spiritual today—to keep that connection. I teach my kids about God, faith, and prayer because I believe it's a fundamental foundation for their lives. I read a lot of scripture, making note of passages that resonate with where I am in my life. I find inspiration in those pages. I still go to church sometimes, usually when I'm trying to figure something out. I'm always looking for a sign in life and often I'll find it there, in the connection that church provides. It's like a reset. I often leave feeling more assured and positive about where I'm heading. It's just about having faith that things will work out. For me, it's incredibly helpful.

I think the faith I learned as a child taught me to understand that there is so much in life that is out of our control. Everything can change in a moment. With my hamstring injury, I felt like everything had changed that quickly.

When I think about it, faith is actually a big part of my training. It's a key element of my psychological approach to performance. It allows me to off-load the concerns and anxieties that can be debilitating. Recentring myself spiritually is kind of like taking a long, deep breath, a pause, when everything around me seems out of control.

During my recovery, I started praying more and showed up to church more often. I had to go back and find myself. It's obviously a spiritual thing, but there is a real psychological component to it too. In those moments of serious doubt about my ability and my future, spending some time reflecting in church or getting away to pray helped me put everything in perspective and calmed my anxiety. It reminded me that everything was going to be okay.

Beyond my hamstring injury, faith has carried me through many rough times in my life. It underpins my understanding of life and purpose and allows me to step back from a very dark place—and to put my trust in a grander vision.

There was a reason I stepped on the bus that day and ran into Mikhile. There was a reason Tony Sharpe happened to be at the track at that exact moment. There was a reason for Coffeyville and

USC. A reason for the Pan Am Games and Rio. It's all part of a plan that I can't possibly comprehend.

Whatever you believe in—even if you're not religious—I think it's helpful to believe in some kind of purpose. There is power in positive thinking. And what's the alternative, really? What is the point in dwelling on the negative? What is the benefit? It only keeps you in a dark place, mentally—and that does nothing to help you overcome life's obstacles. It makes the obstacles seem insurmountable.

Mom still goes to church every Sunday, so I always know I have a prayer going up for me.

But faith alone isn't enough. Dealing with adversity also requires action.

I had to make the decision to keep going, despite feeling like I couldn't. I refused to give up on myself. That was a choice—but it wasn't an easy one.

When I was recovering from my hamstring injury, I prayed a lot. I asked God for strength every day.

There were times within this adversity when I wanted to quit. I felt like I didn't want to do this anymore. I'd put in so much work, only to have everything fall apart with an injury. I had no idea how many times this would happen or whether it would prevent me from ever having success on the track again

Maybe this wasn't for me.

That's where my support system became so crucial. They refused to let me give up on myself.

I was in Toronto through much of my rehab, for about two months. There were some depressing days through that stretch. Every day was a grind. It was like I'd take one step forward and then three steps back. I went through a lot of days like that, where I was like, "Damn, yes. I'm feeling good"—and then all of a sudden, I'd have a setback.

It was during those days that the people around me really supported me. I leaned on Nia, who knew more than anybody what it was like to make a comeback. Nia won gold at the world indoor championships in the 60-metre hurdles in 2014. Then she'd taken a year off to have her son, Titus. Somehow, she managed not only to return to competition in 2016 but also to win the 60-metre hurdles at the world indoor championships again, defending her title. It was an incredible moment. She carried Titus around the track to celebrate.

Nia and I met when we were both training at USC. She had finished going to school by the time I arrived in 2014, but she was still training there. We had all the same coaches, so we kind of got to know each other during that time. But we didn't become friends until 2016—and we got together about a year later. She became one of my biggest inspirations and supports in life. There was nothing I was trying to overcome that she hadn't conquered already.

A lot of people think it's unique that we're both track athletes, but we don't think of it like that. To us, it's just who we are. It's who we've always been as a couple.

At home we don't often talk about track. It's kind of like we leave our work at the office. There is enough going on with our family that we don't have time to talk about it anyway. But when we are training together, we'll give each other advice on how we can improve.

So we definitely study each other's craft. But it's pretty casual.

We both rely on our coach—and so when we do talk about track, there is usually someone in the conversation with us.

It's funny because I hear stories about other couples who are both in the same sport, and they try to avoid training together. They see each other all the time at the house, so they can't work together all day. But that's not the way Nia and I are. We don't get sick of each other like that. We are cool with each other, I guess. We are in this together. When I see her put in work it's inspiring to me. She pushes me to be better. We both have our goals, and we want to see each other achieve them.

And even though we are together a lot, when we're training, when we're competing, we're often apart. I'll be somewhere in Europe, and she'll be getting ready for a different meet in Asia. I'll get home to be with the kids, just as she's getting ready to leave. It's a unique family arrangement, but we find a way to make it work.

Nia was also a huge motivation for me, as she always is. She pushed me to keep going. We were both working on recoveries at the same time. Nia was coming back from having a second baby. *That's* tough. She'd already done it before, so there was no doubt she could do it again.

She had to rebuild her entire core in order to be able to compete. When you're a hurdler your core is everything, so the nature of that physical recovery was incredible. But it's even more amazing because she had to take so much time away from track while she was pregnant and then afterwards. That takes a toll on your fitness. When you don't run for more than a year, you can't just start that engine back up. Your lungs need to get used to that kind of work all over again—let alone the rest of your body.

It's not easy. I see what she goes through. I've seen her

struggle. She's had setbacks along the way. But each time, she knows there is nothing that can stop her. Today, Nia is so mentally strong, it amazes me. More importantly, she inspires and motivates me. She's definitely much stronger than I am. She's shown me that many times. She's tough. She's resilient. Unbreakable.

Nia knows exactly what it's like to tear a hamstring. So when she told me things would get better, I had to believe her.

"You've just got to do the work," Nia would tell me. "Do the work and things will turn around."

And if I wasn't doing the work, one look from Nia and I'd be right back at it. She has more experience than I do. She's been in the sport longer than I have, and she's been through challenges of her own. Nia has gone through all kinds of ups and downs, so she's able to give me advice from her own journey.

Nia also taught me the importance of patience. Patience in the process, and patience in myself. As an athlete, especially a sprinter, I'm so used to rushing forward. But the hamstring injuries forced me to slow down. At times, it made me doubt my future.

"Don't put that negativity in your mind," she'd say. "Things will change, but you've got to get out of your own head."

Your mind is powerful. The things you tell yourself matter. In the most challenging moments, you have to remind yourself that whatever you're struggling with isn't going to last forever. Just as you can't stay on top forever, you won't stay down forever either.

After we had our son in May 2021, I thought Nia was going to be done. She was thinking about retiring. But she has no quit in her. She decided, why the hell not give it one more shot—why not see what I've got left in the tank? "I'm going to keep going," she said. And once again—for a third time—Nia trained incredibly hard just to get back on the track and keep going, this time looking towards the Paris Olympics.

Every day, just being around Nia reminds me that I need to pull myself together. I mean, look what she has overcome as an athlete and in life.

In particular, my relationship with Nia put everything in perspective for me when I was dealing with my hamstring injury. She helped me navigate my rehab by keeping me focused and encouraged. She knew exactly what I was going through.

If Nia could make it back more than once from having a baby, I had nothing to complain about.

And then there was Yuri.

After I'd suffered that second hamstring injury at the Canadian nationals, I flew directly to Philadelphia, where Nia was with her family and our new baby girl. I spent several weeks away from everyone, allowing the strain to heal, while taking my mind off sprinting completely. As frustrated as I was, I knew you never get back the days you miss with your children, especially those early weeks that fly by so quickly. As a new father, I could already feel my world changing.

Even though it felt like everything was falling apart in my career, my baby girl kept me focused on what actually mattered. Every time I held her, I felt an extra rush of motivation. It was a brand new perspective. Now there was someone looking up to me, needing me to be there for them. I can't just be down on myself, feeling devastated, when I have that kind of responsibility in my life.

This gave me a new-found determination to get back to where I was and to be even better.

That year I was fortunate to meet people who could help me get back to where I was determined to be. Matt Nichol was one of those people. A renowned training and conditioning coach in Toronto, Nichol worked with a lot of hockey players. He got his professional start working with the Toronto Maple Leafs before branching off into private practice.

I had to put my faith in people like Matt. I had to trust in his ability—in the reputation he'd earned—to guide me back to where I'd been physically.

Before I could run again, I had to learn to swim. Well, it wasn't really swimming—it was more like walking in water. To build strength without risking further injury, I did exercises on a treadmill inside a small pool at the Canadian Sport Institute Ontario, an athletic training facility at the Toronto Pan Am Sports Centre. Wading through the water, I felt so far away from running 100 metres in under 10 seconds.

Along the way, one of my biggest motivations came from the people who would go out of their way to tell me they'd watched me race in Rio. When I was working out with Matt, several of the other pro athletes who were at his gym at the same time came over to tell me how proud they were to see me on the podium for Canada.

That meant a lot. These were guys who played in the NHL and the NBA, who said they found inspiration just by watching me run. I didn't know what to say. It was a humbling reminder that when I run, I represent my country. People look to athletes in moments of international competition to reflect on collective reasons to be proud of where they come from. The other athletes at Matt's gym encouraged me, telling me how much they wanted to see me back on the track—and eventually back on the podium while the national anthem plays. They told me I made the country proud, which meant a lot to me, especially coming from them.

I believe these people were placed in front of me for a reason. They gave me motivation to keep pushing through rehab despite my disappointment. Through the next year, I focused on building myself back, building that confidence, so I could be there on the podium at the end of the year.

This time I needed to do it the hard way. Instead of trying to get back as quickly as possible, I was going to have to take the time to make sure my hamstring was strong enough not only to compete but also to avoid reinjuring it.

We had to rebuild and retrain the muscle from scratch. But it wasn't the physical training I found difficult; it was the slow process.

Everything needs a foundation. It's like building a house—you've got to start brick by brick. So many people would play an essential part in helping me get back on top physically and mentally. Experts like Matt Nichol, Andy Burke, Chris Klachan, Mark Lindsay, and Alban Merepeza helped guide me through my rehab and comeback. They knew when I needed to push and when I needed to take it light. They forced me to take baby steps, even though I wanted to move as quickly as possible. They knew the importance of that foundation and how to build it properly so I didn't have the same issue again.

The first time, I'd returned too quickly and had been impatient. That's how I ended up getting injured again. This time, I needed to move slowly. But when you move fast for a living, that's a challenge.

I think they could sense my frustration, because they just kept telling me to slow down and trust the process.

"Be patient," they said.

"It's going to come."

"Rome wasn't built in a day."

I would hear all this stuff and fully understand what they were saying. I knew they were right. But some days, my frustration would be obvious. I'd be punching a wall. I'd be like, "Man, this is not working!"

But there was nothing I could do but keep believing.

My goal was to be back in peak form in time for the World Championships in Doha in September 2019—more than two years since I'd first suffered that injury ahead of the worlds in London.

That journey didn't suddenly become easy.

I had to get off my couch and stop being down on myself. I had to stop feeling sorry for myself, thinking my career was done. That kind of motivation doesn't just happen once and then you're good. I had to work at it. I had to get up every day and tell myself to move forward. Some days were easier than others. Moving through adversity is a journey of peaks and valleys. There are going to be very difficult days on the way to where you need to be.

One of the key things I had to do was remind myself how much life lay ahead for me. I turned 24 years old that fall. My life was far from over, but an athlete's career is short. I had to tell myself there was still plenty of time to reach my goals.

I realized during this time how necessary it is to have the right people around you as you fight through adversity.

The people helping me through this, like Chris, Andy, Matt, and Alban, were great at keeping me focused on the positive. They reminded me that I still have lots of time to build my legacy in the sport. This was a frustrating setback, but not the end.

Mentors like Anson Henry and several others were also very important to me during this time. Anson struggled with injuries throughout his career. He knew exactly what I was going through, so I leaned on his advice and wisdom. Anson reminded me that if I wanted to get back to where I was before, the first thing to do was get out of my own head and stay mentally strong.

This became a particularly key message when I got to a point where my hamstring was healed and I'd built back my strength. Matt had done a great job helping me get into a position to perform physically—but I was still hesitant on the track. I wasn't myself. When I'd run, I'd worry I was about to tear my hamstring again. I was hesitant, and in sprinting you can't flinch. This enormous barrier was harder to overcome than the injury itself because the remedy wasn't clear.

Anson reminded me that I already knew what it would take to get back. I knew it was a mental game. My injury was healed, so I needed to have confidence in that.

"The doctor cleared you and said, 'You're fine,'" Anson reminded me. "Now it's really just about putting in that work."

It wasn't just people I knew either. I'd run into complete strangers who'd tell me they were proud of how I'd represented the country and they couldn't wait to see me get back on the track. People sent kind messages to me through social media. Everyone wanted to help or encourage me in some way.

The support was overwhelming. I received so much motivation from all kinds of people reaching out to encourage me to keep grinding. So many people believed it was going to come together. That helped me believe it actually would.

I was lucky to be able to see that kind of support directly because

I was in the public spotlight. Most people don't have strangers reaching out to them encouraging them through their biggest challenges. But even with that attention, I could still find myself feeling alone through these struggles. I think it's helpful for anyone facing adversity to remind themselves that they are not alone. People are rooting for you. People believe in you. I know most people don't receive kind messages on social media or have random strangers offer support. Still, you're never alone—remember there *are* people who are rooting for you. There are people who believe in you. Even if it's just one person you can trust. Surround yourself with people who seek to build you up. We tear ourselves down enough on our own, so we don't need any help with that. Block out the negative voices, and find comfort in the encouragement of others.

Getting quality advice and guidance helped me believe I was on my way back. I had some of the top minds in the industry working on my behalf. It gave me confidence in the process, which is valuable when you're dealing with something that has such a strong psychological layer. Without that support, I don't think I would have been able to get my career back on track.

Eventually, I started to feel like myself again. I started to really believe. All of that faith turned into action—and the results came.

When I arrived in Doha for the 2019 World Championships in September, it was effectively my big return after two years of working to recover from my hamstring injury. The entire season, as I gradually got better, was a lead-up to the worlds. I'd reached the podium six times in eight races since my return in May, regaining the confidence and swagger I'd felt two years earlier, back in the summer of 2017. It felt like it had been an eternity. For a sprinter, that's pretty much what it was.

It took a hell of a lot of patience to get there.

When I lined up in the 100-metre final in Doha, I knew I needed to lay it all out on the track. This was my moment. I stood on the line beside the best in the world, knowing it would be a great race.

I didn't win gold that day. I took the bronze behind Christian Coleman and Justin Gatlin. But I ran a personal best 9.90, a hair faster than my bronze-medal performance in Rio. I was back. It felt great to finally be there. Nia, Yuri, and my mother were in the stands, cheering me on. I couldn't have asked for more.

"Moving forward, I know I can get better," I told the CBC's Scott Russell after the race.

Three days later, I tapped my chest and pointed up to the sky right before getting set in the blocks for the 200-metre final.

The gun fired. I held a good pace but was behind coming off the bend. As the line neared, I felt a familiar burst rising within me. The final stretch belonged to me. I felt no fear—no concern that I'd break down and wind up back where I started. I was there to finish this part of my journey. I took off through the final 40 metres. I felt a slight rush of fatigue in the final 10—almost like a reminder of where I'd been. But that was behind me now.

I finished just behind Noah Lyles in 19.95 to claim the silver.

Draped in a Canadian flag, I tapped my chest three times and pointed up. It was an incredible relief. I was back.

Again Scott Russell spoke with me for the CBC as I was still catching my breath. He asked me about winning silver and a goal I'd set to land on the podium.

"If you asked me this question a year ago, I didn't think I would be here," I said. "I'm happy. I'm blessed to get back to where I was. And next year is going to be an incredible year for me, I believe."

Russell noted how happy and relaxed I seemed while getting back to business. He asked me what the biggest factor had been for me.

"Family," I said. "They motivated me, inspired me, and pushed me to come back from my injuries. A lot of faith in God. Just trying to tell myself to leave it all in his plan, and I'm going to be back better than ever."

I meant every word.

Nia, my mother, my friends—my inner circle of support—were so essential during that time. They kept telling me this was all part of the process. They reminded me I'd never been through anything like this before but that I would make it through, and that I'd be stronger for it. One day, I'd feel like I was on top of the world again. One day, I'd know I'd conquered something special.

The lessons I learned through those hardest days will be lessons I'll carry for the rest of my life. Whatever adversity I face next, I'll be ready. I now know I can conquer anything.

A week later, Nia won gold in the 100-metre hurdles, marking her own incredible comeback 16 months after giving birth to our daughter. As if we needed another reason to believe that with faith and action, anything is possible.

I firmly believe there is power in faith—however a person might find it. We gain strength from knowing we have a purpose and a destiny. There is little value in allowing ourselves to be overcome by doubt. I say that as someone who clearly felt a lot of doubt at times. But I felt weakest when I allowed my faith to waver. It's a lesson I've had to learn many times. A lesson I know I will likely relearn on many more occasions.

If you are facing an obstacle in your life, what is the value in telling yourself you can't get past it? Those thoughts only work against you.

But on the other side, belief alone isn't enough. I couldn't just sit at my house believing I'd one day make it back to the podium. I had to move on that faith. I had to act.

When we set out to achieve something—whether it be an obstacle or a goal—we put ourselves at an advantage when we are able to cultivate a mindset geared to success. Believing you deserve to achieve that goal, whether by destiny or will, is so important. But without a deliberate, constant effort to achieve it, that goal will never be reached.

22

SLOW DOWN

When I battled my hamstring injury, I missed a lot of the season trying to rest and recover fully. That time away from the track came at a cost. I missed out on a lot of paydays because I wasn't able to compete. I was supporting just myself at the time, so I didn't worry about it too much. I didn't have a family to think about, so I had the ability to go without for a while in order to get back to where I needed to be. Of course, it ended up being nearly two years of limited competition because the rehabilitation process took so long.

Healing properly was a luxury. But the reality was that my anxiety about wanting to get back to competing wasn't just about my desire to win and be the fastest in the world. It was also about earning a living.

A lot of people don't know about the realities of life as a track athlete. I'm fortunate to have signed a contract with Puma, which changed my life. But there are obligations that come with contracts, because of course a partner like Puma is investing in me because they want to align their brand with how I perform. If I'm not performing, Puma doesn't get the same value out of our partnership.

That's the business.

As much as I love sports, this is how I make my living. This is how I provide for my family. But it's a career that exists for a limited time. There will come a day when I will no longer be able to run as fast as I do now. That's inevitable. So I need to plan not only for today but for the decades to come, because I am lucky to have an opportunity to do that now.

It's a blessing, but it also comes with a great deal of pressure.

When I tour on circuits like the Diamond League and compete at other pro meets, I'm fortunate to be able to earn an appearance fee because of the profile I've built. When I first started out, I wasn't able to earn a fee just for showing up, and many athletes on the circuit don't. Winning a prestigious event like that will earn a runner in the ballpark of $10,000. That's a lot of money. But if you think about it, to earn $50,000 in a year you need to win five events. That's not easy to do. And that's a lot of pressure to earn a decent living.

And even when things are going well, like when you've reached the podium at the World Championships or at the Olympics, you're one bad season or one injury away from losing everything. It doesn't matter who you are. If you're not competing and you're not drawing fans, your value plummets.

I want to be clear: I am not complaining about that. My track career has given me a life I could have only dreamed of when I was younger. I'm so grateful to be able to do what I do. But for every athlete—each dealing with a ticking clock in their career—there is a constant pressure to compete, which can be at odds with the need to recover so you can actually reach your potential each season. It's an endless tension.

Being a pro in some sports, like hockey and basketball, allows players to continue to get paid while they are recovering from an injury. It's guaranteed money. That doesn't mean they are fully protected, of course. An injury can still affect their ability to earn their next contract. But they don't get paid per game in the same way a track athlete is paid per appearance—or per win. The financial reality is different.

In track, that can play a role in the decisions you make throughout your career. You need to be very careful because every decision has a consequence. You need to have a sense of what the outcome will be. If I miss several events in a row, what will that mean for my reputation? Will promoters be less interested in having me come to their event if I've missed months trying to heal from an injury?

During the two years I battled through injuries, that was a reality for me. I could try to compete at an event to earn a decent paycheque, but what if I were to get injured again? Would that jeopardize my ability to perform at my best at the World Championships and Olympic Games? Was it worth it?

The other factor is that athletes' contracts often require them to compete in a certain number of events each year. I need to make appearances because that's my job as an ambassador of a world-class brand like Puma. When I don't run it means I'm not meeting those obligations. I'm very grateful for the partnership I've had with Puma through my career, but it's not like I'm just able to sign with them and that's it. There are responsibilities I need to honour as part of that commitment. They want people to see me running in their shoes in person and on TV. They want me to compete— and to win.

I have a team that works very closely on my behalf, including my track agent Paul and my marketing agent Brian. Having a team like that supporting me is a huge benefit.

Each of the opportunities I'm given in these areas comes with responsibilities, which I take very seriously. It's all part of the job of a professional athlete. There is much more to think about than running alone.

Through the ups and downs of my career, I've learned that you have to choose your battles. I need to play the long game. I have to keep in mind the totality of my career and how the decisions I make today will affect me in the months and years to come.

From a competition perspective, that means deciding whether I will run a race, even though I know I won't be at my best, in order to fulfill contractual commitments or collect an appearance fee. So I can rest or I can collect a bit of money and avoid getting a reduction in my contract because I didn't meet a threshold number of appearances. These pro events are key when it comes to my endorsement deals in particular because at major events in which I represent Canada, like the Olympics and World Championships, I'll wear the national team kit. So the brands I partner with don't get the same kind of exposure because I can't wear their logos on my uniform while competing, but I still wear my Puma spikes. Puma is also a sponsor of some meets, which adds another consideration for the meets I race in.

I signed a second contract with Puma in 2020, which runs through to the end of 2023. There are special performance-based bonuses written into contracts like that, so the better I perform the more I'm rewarded. For example, winning gold in Tokyo unlocked a bonus clause in my deal.

Endorsement deals like this are actually how track athletes make most of their money, aside from racing for prize money, which is hard to survive on alone. Without the support of these brands, it would be very difficult to have the freedom to treat the sport like a full-time job, as an athlete needs to if they are going to perform at their best. The stuff I do off the track with sponsors like GoDaddy, Gatorade, and Subway is far from the norm for most track athletes. And I also have to carry myself well and be careful, because one wrong move in public could tarnish my reputation and put those relationships in jeopardy.

Appearance fees take some stress out of competing at track meets around the world, but it's usually only World Championship and Olympic medallists who receive those. And that's never a guarantee. It's all about the perceived draw. Nia, my girlfriend, wasn't able to get appearance fees until she won an Olympic medal in 2016. But after that—in part because she took time off to be a mother—Nia stopped being offered appearance fees. It wasn't until her remarkable return at the 2019 World Championships, after having our daughter, Yuri, that Nia started to receive appearance fees again.

An agent will negotiate with the organizers of the meet, which is usually arranged based on ticket sales and sponsorships, because people are coming to watch you compete in their event. I've been fortunate to get appearance fees because I won Olympic medals in 2016 and 2021. Those victories lead to more respect, global exposure, and therefore more leverage.

Truthfully, if it were up to me, I wouldn't want to run unless I was always at my best. But I need to fulfill certain requirements because the money isn't guaranteed. For example, I have to stay near the top of the world rankings, and in order to stay near the top, you need to run races. The more time you take off, the more your ranking slides.

So when you take time to recover, it costs you. But if you want to compete and be at your best, you need to take time to recover. If you don't, you won't perform well and could risk serious injury, which would cost you even more.

Now that I have children, I am much more aware of this reality. If I still had to take care of just myself, I don't think I would feel the same amount of pressure. I can take a loss in a situation like that. But my kids need me. If you're a parent, you know this. I have a chance to create a great life for them, and I don't want to miss any opportunity to better secure their future. I plan to have a career beyond track, of course, but this is my time to earn my living as a professional athlete. Everything else, right now, is unknown and unpredictable.

When the COVID pandemic hit, the precarious nature of what I do as a professional athlete became very apparent. The pandemic hammered so many people's lives in ways I can't possibly understand, so I don't want to compare my concerns with those of anyone who lost a loved one or had to struggle as the world ground to a halt.

There were the same concerns everyone was dealing with, of people getting sick and dying around the world. Every day it seemed like the news was getting worse and the world was shutting down. Where was everything heading? It all seemed almost apocalyptic. There was so much uncertainty. So much tragedy.

It was scary. Track was obviously secondary to those concerns.

The pandemic threw *everyone's* life off balance. But it also affected each of us in different ways. For me—and many athletes—the pandemic meant our ability to compete, perform, and earn a living was put on hold.

When everything shut down, it meant I wasn't able to train and all our upcoming meets were cancelled. The kind of preparation I'd normally do ahead of an event like the Olympics was impossible. One of the biggest obstacles initially was the uncertainty around whether the 2020 Games in Tokyo would even take place.

As professional sports leagues and major events shuttered one by one, the IOC and the Tokyo Olympics organizing committee remained determined that the Games would go on as planned. But as the pandemic continued, it seemed less and less likely that the Olympics could take place. There was all kinds of speculation, which was difficult on athletes who were struggling to find ways to train as the world shut down and had no idea when or if they would be able to compete. On March 23, 2020, the Canadian Olympic Committee was the first national body to announce it would pull out of the Tokyo Games unless they were postponed for a year. Australia did the same shortly after. It was the beginning of a domino effect of resistance from nations and athletes that eventually pushed the IOC and Tokyo organizing committee to postpone the Games by a year, to July 2021.

The decision offered little reassurance. It was still unclear how we'd effectively be able to prepare—or whether the Olympics would take place at all, amid all the uncertainty of where the pandemic was heading. There were so many unknowns.

How do you get ready to compete in the Olympics if you can't even train? What if I got out of shape? What time frame were we working with? Could the Games actually take place in 2021? Who knew how long the world would be shut down for?

For Olympic athletes the pandemic put years of training and planning in limbo. For so many, the Games represent years of personal and financial sacrifice. There are not many Olympic sports that bring in lucrative contracts or winnings. Most athletes compete at great sacrifice because of their passion and dedication. They would need to sacrifice further, and some would miss out on a chance to compete altogether.

The transition was difficult. I went from a consistent schedule, travelling from meet to meet in locations around the world, to struggling to find a track near my home in Florida where I'd be allowed to run.

For a while we weren't even able to do that. The university where I trained in Jacksonville, Florida, shut down. All the local high schools were closed too. Eventually, we managed to gain access to a public football turf. A person we knew allowed us to use his private gym to work out. After a while we found a public high school track that no one seemed inclined to prevent us from using. It was a beat-up gravel track about 20 minutes from where I lived. It was the kind that usually circles an overgrown football or soccer field, without any lines or markers to indicate distance. That track became one of my main training sites for months.

I had only one track event in 2020. A group was able to organize an event in Florida, in which we lined up with only three people on the track at the time, to adhere to social distancing guidelines. I was lucky enough to be able to make $10,000 at the meet because I won the race—but other than that, I didn't really make any money that year outside of endorsements.

And those faded quickly too.

I know how fortunate I am to compete in an Olympic sport in which it is possible to earn a nice living. The attention paid to sprinting globally gave me a chance to make a great living as an athlete. I know I have it better than most, and I don't want to compare the impact the pandemic had on me with the experience of those athletes who, despite being the best in the word, have not had the same privilege.

But the reality is that in order to make a good living in track, I've had to work hard to build and retain relationships and partnerships with brands that align with what I value as a person and as an athlete.

By 2020, I'd learned a lot about the business side of track. During the recovery from my hamstring injury, the money I made from sponsors could have dwindled. It made sense, of course. It's a business and if I can't run—If I'm not seen—then I'm not as valuable. I learned how quickly that can happen.

But I also learned the value of strong partnerships with brands that value long-term relationships. In 2018, my marketing agent Brian had a meeting scheduled with Gatorade, in which he worried the company was planning to back out of our partnership, one of my longest standing, because I hadn't been able to compete well and ended another season early with an injury. Instead, they reaffirmed their belief in what I could still achieve and signed me for a longer deal. It was an act of faith I'll never forget. During a difficult time, Gatorade was willing to stand by me. That meant so much for my confidence when I needed it. To this day, I still have a Gatorade fridge stocked with drinks.

The experience of losing partnerships during my injury prepared me for what the pandemic would bring, from a business perspective. Without events to compete in, my income went down. In addition, world-altering events like a pandemic hadn't been considered in my endorsement contracts, which meant I didn't have full paycheques coming in.

All of my contracts were cut in some capacity. Some partnerships were more generous than others, only cutting about 20 percent of my pay. Of course, I understood this reality. These companies were dealing with a pandemic too.

But it was a struggle financially. There was the immediate hit, but also the uncertainty. It was unclear whether any of these contracts would come back. I didn't know if I'd ever be able to earn the living I had before.

Brian was able to arrange some virtual event appearances for me where I'd log in to a digital town hall meeting and do my best to inspire staff through a moderated question and answer session. Those speaking gigs brought in some money, which I was grateful for. But it was also inspiring to see sponsors find creative ways to utilize athletes through the pandemic. In early 2020, Cheerios boxes with images of me and other Canadian Olympic athletes were already being distributed ahead of the Tokyo Olympics. But Cheerios flipped the focus of the campaign to support food banks, which saw a large spike in usage amid the Covid-19 crisis. They made a series of videos with me and other Olympians sharing the personal stories of food bank workers, who were the true heroes of the time.

At the same time, my initial contract with Puma was up for renewal. I didn't know what to expect. Would they want to continue working with me? Would they still see the value in our partnership? I hoped so. We had a great relationship. I believed in the brand, and I knew they believed in me. But it was by no means certain. Nothing was certain anymore.

Up to that point, my hamstring injury had been the toughest obstacle in my career. I thought I had conquered that. After such a long grind, I was ready to move forward. The pandemic knocked me back into a place of doubt and uncertainty. I was in my prime, and it felt like time was running out.

Over the previous two years I'd discovered a resilience in me that I didn't know existed. It was a spirit I didn't know I needed until I faced a potentially career-altering injury. I now had the tools to step back and put the pandemic and its effect on my life and career into perspective.

///////

Despite the obvious setbacks, there were blessings that came with the pandemic. My life hadn't ceased the constant rush forward since I'd stood on that line back at York University as a kid, with no clear future and no plan for where the race would take me. For all the benefits that life had brought me, it had taken a toll too. These things always do. I had been on the move ever since I'd found a reason to dream I could accomplish something special. But we aren't built for that. No one can sprint through their entire life. And no one should want to.

Throughout my injury, I kept pushing forward, trying to get back into the endless race. But the pandemic made me stop. For the first time, I couldn't move forward. As the world I'd built around me shook and fractured, I was able to see the pieces that truly mattered.

I spent more time at home, alongside Nia, enjoying the life we had built together. It was a life of frenetic pace . . . suddenly still. I hung out with my stepson, Titus, watching superhero movies and sharing our mutual love of sports. I took time to hold our daughter, Yuri. I watched her grow. I watched her smile and laugh and saw the wonder of this world expand in her eyes. It was beautiful.

The uncertainty of the pandemic became an opportunity. I was able to spend more time with my family and to get exhausted by them, in the way every parent should. I was able to reflect on why I do what I do. It's not just for the love of the sport or the thrill of competition. I do what I do because of the people I love.

I run for them.

Amid the pandemic, I was able to remind myself of that foundational fact.

With my training, finances, and entire career facing an uncertainty I simply couldn't imagine even through two years battling a hamstring injury, I found an opportunity to stop and reassess what I'm pursuing. Why do I run at all?

There are many reasons why I do what I do, of course. But the reason I run is for the time spent beyond the finish line. It's for the moments between those brief blurs of speed, when I am just Andre De Grasse—a friend, a son, a partner, a father. A man trying to find his path, in a world where that seems increasingly hard to do.

Through all that doubt, I found more certainty in who I am, and why I do what I do, than I ever had before.

And those reasons were only getting stronger.

In May 2021, Nia and I welcomed our son, Kenzo, to the world. My purpose grew.

At the same time, the world started to slowly open up again. Track and field events returned in Europe, showing a way back to how things were. Then they returned in the United States, first in small markets. Big-market events soon followed, which meant the path to financial and professional security started to reopen.

Looking back, I can see what I gained when everything slowed down. It was frustrating and hard at times, but I ended up with a perspective I didn't have before.

///////

I don't know how the pandemic affected you and your family. I know for many it brought hardships I can't comprehend. But I believe that amid the most difficult and uncertain times in our lives, there is opportunity.

Why do *you* do what you do? Why do you wake up each morning and pursue the life you lead? What is *your* purpose? In the midst of our biggest challenges, facing our greatest doubts, we find the most revealing answers.

So many of us spend our days speeding past the good parts of life, moving from one obligation to the next. In a fast life it's easy to lose focus on why we're running in the first place. Forced to come to an almost complete stop, I was able to take a look around and remind myself what the pace is for—and that sometimes it's okay to just slow down.

23

THE RACE OF MY LIFE

The privilege I've been given to represent Canada at the Olympics is an enormous responsibility.

People always used to remind me: "You're here, representing your country—few people get the chance to do this."

That always makes me feel filled with purpose. I'm one of the few. I need to make the most of it.

I recently watched *Spider-Man* with my stepson and it reminded me of that feeling. It was funny. I heard that famous line: "With great power comes great responsibility."

That's how I view the opportunities I've been blessed with. It's how I think we all should view the opportunities our individual talents and abilities give us. We all have our own great powers—and we all have our own responsibilities.

When I get set on the blocks, I feel responsible to make the most of the gifts I've been given. Let's be real: I stumbled into sprinting. It wasn't my plan. It was almost like a scene from a movie, where suddenly a character realizes, by accident, that they have special power.

It matters how I use that power. If I don't do everything I can to make the most of it, then I've wasted it. If I don't do everything possible to use it for something good, then I've taken it for granted and missed the entire point.

Whenever I speak to kids, I encourage them to believe in the special gifts they've been given and to use those powers for good.

At the Tokyo Olympics, I felt like it was my responsibility to make my country proud. That's a big weight to carry, but it's how I felt. If I was going to lead, I had to conquer this challenge. I'd won three Olympic medals at the Rio Olympics. It'd been five long, difficult years to get to this moment—with a chance to claim gold.

I had to conquer that challenge. It was my only goal.

But I was also pragmatic about it. I knew what I wanted to achieve, and I had done the work to put myself in a position to achieve it. But competition is unpredictable. You can only do so much until fate takes over. What is meant to be will happen. At least that's what I believe.

I've always told myself that you've got to live with the results. So you go out there and you give it your all. You give it 100 percent. Whatever happens, happens. That simple philosophy is always in the back of my mind, which I think helps me deal with the inevitable disappointments that come with a career like mine.

In big moments like the Olympics, when I feel the weight of enormous expectation, I've learned to compartmentalize.

Obviously, everyone's paying attention. I want strangers I've never met to feel pride as Canadians. I want to inspire kids who are watching to believe they can do things that might seem impossible. I want to lead with the gift I've been given.

But to process that, I think about my family—my inner circle. They are the most important people in my life. The people who have stood by me through so many ups and downs in this journey. So when I think of the pressure, when I think of who is watching, I think of them.

/////

I was confident going into the 100-metre final in August at the Olympic Stadium in Tokyo.

I looked across the line and knew I could beat everyone else there—knew that I *had* beaten everyone there before.

This was my chance to finally get the gold medal that escaped me at the Rio Games five years earlier. In Tokyo I had a chance to become the third Canadian to win Olympic gold in the 100 metres, along with Percy Williams in 1928 and Donovan Bailey in 1996.

I felt good in the blocks—relaxed and focused—but a false start by Zharnel Hughes got in my head a bit. I didn't want to lose my chance by starting too quickly after he was shown the red card and disqualified from the race. That's the last thing you want on that stage. But you also don't want to tense up on the blocks, worrying about a false start.

When the gun went off again, I hesitated. It was the worst start of the entire field in the 100-metre final. It was by far the worst start I'd had in the 100 in Tokyo. All I could do was make up ground. I had to catch the field.

"This is going to be a tough one," I thought.

I had to chase the footsteps pounding ahead of me. I had to

make up for lost time. I knew I wasn't where I wanted to be, but I didn't panic. It was a position I'd been in many times before: starting behind and then building speed. I reached another level through the final stretch. I felt myself coming back, coming back, coming back—but I just ran out of track.

I'd flown to the finish, but it wasn't enough. I caught most of them before the line, all except for Lamont Marcell Jacobs of Italy and Fred Kerley from the United States.

Our times flashed onscreen above us. The Italian shocked us all, but none of us had ever run that fast before. Across the podium, we each ran a personal best. It's amazing that even though we pushed ourselves so many times before, when the stakes were at the highest we found a way to move at a speed that had not previously been attainable. Human capability is remarkable that way.

My best just wasn't *the* best. Not that day anyway. My time of 9.89 was enough to earn my fourth Olympic medal, my first in Tokyo. I've watched that race many times since, trying to figure out what exactly went wrong. It seems strange to try to figure out what went wrong when I had actually run faster than I ever had before—but that's the nature of this sport. You're never fully satisfied with your best. As long as someone else is faster, you need to believe you can be faster too.

I think that's a fundamental element in the pursuit of excellence. Even when you achieve something you've worked hard for, part of you should be able to celebrate that and find joy in it. But another part of you, the relentlessly competitive perfectionist part of you, knows you could do better. The balance between both, I think, is crucial. You don't want to be so competitive that you can't be happy with a personal best and a podium finish at the Olympics.

There is so much to celebrate there. But if you're not standing at the top of the podium there is always that sting—that reminder that someone else is there instead of you. I think that is part of the drive for greatness. You need to feel you're going to continue to improve. You have to believe that you can. You have to want it with every part of you.

I'd added another Olympic medal to my count. It was a win. But I left the track that day wanting more.

In the 200-metre final three days later, on August 4, the pursuit of that elusive medal was a key storyline heading into the race.

"Andre De Grasse—so often the 'nearly' man. Is it his turn this time?" wondered the commentator on the international Olympic broadcast, as the camera panned across me. My family and close friends watched from my mother's living room back in Pickering, where it was morning. Usually they would have been in the stands cheering me on, but the pandemic meant that most of the venue's 68,000 seats were empty. In Tokyo, I stood alone in what might have felt like an eerie silence if I hadn't been so locked in on the steps ahead.

I'd faced so many big moments before, but this was by far the most important race of my life. I was considered a contender, but by no means was I guaranteed a spot on the podium, let alone a gold medal.

I was going to have to be my best. But I wasn't as confident as I had been before the 100-metre final. I didn't have the same sense that I could win it. My competition was tough. Noah Lyles, the 2019 world champion, was one of the front-runners. His fellow Americans Kenneth Bednarek and Erriyon Knighton, who was just 17, were also both threats. And of course, my Canadian teammate

Aaron Brown was dangerous too. We'd team up in the 4 x 100-metre relay, but beside each other on the line we were long-time competitors. I had no intention of taking a step back for him.

I was in lane six, between Bednarek and Knighton. Lyles was in lane three. Aaron in lane four.

Even though they are both sprints, the 100 and 200 are two very different races.

I enjoy the 100 metres best. There isn't as much thinking involved. You start in the same position as everyone else. It's pure force to the finish line. You run your fastest right through. In the 100 you feel people beside you. You hear the rumble of their footsteps, and you can see their blur in your peripheral vision, if you're not ahead. But you can't see exactly who you are racing or who is leading or who is behind. It's a mass of bodies that you have raced before, studied before, but in that moment you're in your lane and it's just you against the world, chasing you down.

The 200 metres is much more complicated.

It's harder to train for, especially for me. The workouts are tough, causing a rapid buildup of lactic acid in my muscles that becomes very painful. Sometimes we'll do longer distances to prepare for the 200—running 300 or 400 metres, just to build that extra endurance. I often find those days gruelling. Training for both events is especially difficult, but my goal is to be the best in both and so I refuse to give either up, at least at this point in my career.

So the journey to get to the line in an Olympic 200-metre final is already taxing. The race itself requires much more thought and strategy. It's probably more conducive to my style of running. I'm not as quick out of the blocks as many of my competitors, but my top-end speed is faster than theirs. So with more distance to make up ground, I can pass most runners who've started ahead as I reach my peak speed—kind of like the Road Runner zipping past Wile E. Coyote.

In the 200 everything shifts on the turn off the bend of the first 100 metres. I want to put myself in a good position coming out of the first half of the race, but I don't necessarily need to hold a lead at that point. The turn is like a slingshot—you want to rocket out of the corner. And then you hit a peak speed, hopefully faster than everyone else. It's all downhill from there. You just want to maintain that speed through the finish line.

To the outside world, it happens in a flash. But on the track it's much different. You can see others in your peripheral vision, but just like a blur beside you. And you can hear the sounds of the spikes hitting the ground around you. You can hear someone coming up on you, literally breathing down your neck. It's hard to explain how you know where you stand in a race—how you know how much more you need to give. It's a feeling, a blend of seeing and hearing. It's almost instinctual. You just know.

In Tokyo that night, I felt it right away. Off the gun, I knew I had a decent jump. Everything just felt natural. Everything was quiet. Just spikes on the track, the breath of others, and the peripheral blur.

Sometimes in the race you kind of feel your legs are getting heavy—you can feel the lactic acid building. You're like, "Come on! I've got to keep going." But it's a grind from the start. Those are the races you don't want.

But that night I didn't feel tight; I was relaxed. My legs were just flowing. The first 100 metres was a battle for position. When I came off the turn, I didn't feel any weight in my legs. I just felt my legs moving up and down, up and down—symmetrical, just moving swiftly. Moving in flow and rhythm.

I knew it was going to be a good race. I felt a burst of strength. I felt upright and powerful.

"I have a chance to win this," I thought. "I'm about to have the race of my life."

At the turn, you're always looking at who you need to pass, because that's where the distances of the staggered start even out. Anyone ahead of you at that moment has the edge.

The only guy I saw ahead of me was Kenneth Bednarek, in the lane beside me. But he didn't have enough space to hold on to his lead. He was close and I was going to catch him. I was within hunting distance. I was close enough to him that I could get him to tighten up. He'd feel me coming. He'd hear my footsteps and it would make him freeze up.

On the stretch, I felt more power driving through my legs. I was flying. I'd never felt that way in my life. Even when I'd set personal bests in the past, I hadn't noticed how well I was doing until afterwards. But that night I felt like I was about to run faster than I ever had.

I knew I'd won when I got to about 180 metres. I felt myself taking over, passing Bednarek through the final 10 to 15 metres. Once I knew I passed him, it was game over. There was no way that Noah Lyles in lane three was about to pass me. I didn't feel him. I didn't see him. I didn't hear him. Once I caught Bednarek, it was me versus the clock.

I crossed the line and looked up.

19.62

Gold.

I'd done it.

I let out a roar.

"Let's go!" I shouted to empty seats, throwing my hands up as if gesturing to a screaming crowd. And I just kept running as the moment processed. I slowed down and looked up, hands resting on my forehead. Then I fell to my knees and crumpled over onto the track, covering my head. I let out several heaves, as though I was panting for air. I was exhausted. More exhausted than I'd felt before—a mix of physical and emotional shock. I rolled over onto my back, realizing I'd just run a personal best, another Canadian record. And an Olympic gold medal. The first Canadian to win the 200 at the Olympics in nearly a century, since Percy Williams in 1928.

I got back up as Noah came over to shake my hand and give me a hug. Then I wandered the track trying to take it in. I saw the camera following me so I looked into it and shouted "I love you" to everyone in my world who had made this moment possible. We had come so far and been so close—and now we were on top of the world.

Someone asked if I needed water. I did—I really, really did. Another person handed me a giant Canadian flag, which I draped around my shoulders. My heart pounded. I tried to catch my breath.

I walked up to a screen that had been set up to broadcast the families of athletes to the track, so they could share in the moment.

My daughter Yuri was jumping up and down.

"Yuri! Did you see me?" I asked.

She kept on cheering and jumping. I'd made her proud. It was the greatest moment of my life.

24

IT TAKES A TEAM

Winning gold at the Tokyo Olympics in the summer of 2021 was the biggest moment of my career. The victory was bittersweet, given everything I'd overcome to get there. Two years earlier, I wasn't sure if I'd be able to continue running at all. As wonderful as it felt to cross that line first, it was also a bit lonely because the people who had supported me through all of the ups and downs weren't able to be there to experience it with me in person.

They watched from the other side of the world. Shortly after my victory, CBC anchor Adrienne Arsenault handed me her phone, with everyone who gathered at my mother's house back in Canada on FaceTime. Hearing their cheers through the phone made the memory complete. These were the people whose love and support made my Olympic gold medal possible. It was the most amazing moment to share, even if we were a world apart.

The truth is we don't achieve anything alone.

I've learned to lean on my support system when things aren't going right. Without the people in my corner, I probably wouldn't have been able to get through some of the toughest periods of my career.

It doesn't matter what you are chasing in life. If you set goals for yourself, you are much more likely to achieve them if you've got people in your corner who are not only cheering for you but also supporting you in the pursuit of those goals. I'm not just talking about friends and acquaintances. I believe we set ourselves up for success when we know we can rely on a specific group of people to provide wisdom, advice, support, tough love, and encouragement when we need it most.

Be thoughtful about who you select to be part of your inner circle.

Things don't always go as planned. The past few years certainly taught me that lesson. Through times of uncertainty—like injuries and the pandemic—I learned the importance of leaning on your inner circle for support. For me, that inner circle is made up of family, friends, and supporters who have always been there, regardless of what's happening in my life.

The season that followed Olympic gold brought another serious setback.

I suffered a foot injury in training in the spring of 2022, which nagged me for the entire year. I had to fly to Toronto to get treatment first, trying to rehabilitate the injury without missing too much of the season, which included the World Championships in Oregon that July. The injury prevented me from being able to accelerate off the blocks, which was just enough of a disadvantage to lead to several disappointing finishes in a row. A bout with

COVID then held me out of competition and training for weeks and left me feeling sluggish even after I'd recovered.

I was so frustrated. It was déjà vu.

I'd just come off my best Olympic performance, winning gold in Tokyo—and less than a year later, I was injured. It felt like 2017 all over again.

I went from having the greatest season of my career to having the worst start to a season yet. It was a harsh reminder that you can't stay on top forever. When I dealt with those struggles through the 2022 season, it reminded me how difficult it was in 2017 and 2018, when there were days I thought I might never make it back. The same doubts I'd quietly carried throughout my career crept back into my mind: *Maybe I'll never be the same.*

It's important for each of us to remember that even when we've achieved success, there will always be new challenges to overcome.

I know that, but that doesn't mean I'm immune to getting down on myself and getting stuck in a rut. Sometimes you need people to tell you to "Get back up and keep going." I think everybody needs that. It's just part of being human.

When you surround yourself with positive, wonderful people, they lift your spirits. That's what keeps you going. That's what puts a smile on your face.

Dealing with yet another setback in my career, I leaned into the help of the support group around me. With their encouragement, I was able to take a breath and remember how I felt the first time—how the doubt consumed me. Four years later, I became the Olympic champion. I'd proved all the doubters, including that part of myself, wrong.

I needed to remember that.

What happened in those four years? How was I able to overcome it?

As I wrote earlier there were a few things: Faith, action, and determination were essential. But underpinning all of that were the people surrounding me.

Once again, my girlfriend Nia was the most important among them. She was on me constantly, encouraging me through my toughest days. She reminded me about how much I'd sacrificed to get to the position I was in. She reminded me of the constant work I had put in, and of the faith I'd found within myself—that belief that I was going to make it back, despite the lingering doubts.

"Keep having that faith in yourself and things are going to turn around," Nia said.

My mother was also one of my biggest encouragers, as she's always been. After I won gold in Tokyo, she told the CBC that she'd been worried about the pressure I felt heading into the Games.

"I know how hard he's trained for this," she said. "To hear him say that he had the weight of the whole world on his shoulders? No one should have to go through that. . . . He was doing this for everybody, the country, his family—I mean, that's such a difficult thing to ask of anybody."

Mom knew how tough I'd been on myself through that long journey to get back to the top. She knew about the pressure and the doubt I felt. She knew how badly I wanted to make my country proud. Mom was thrilled to see me win gold. She called it the best day of her life. But she also knew that, despite my joy, I wouldn't be satisfied. She knew there were valleys to come.

"All the pressure that is being put on them to really perform," she told the CBC. "Is it really worth all of this?"

Back in a valley less than a year later, as I stayed at her place and worked through rehab on my foot, my mother once again saw the frustration and doubt. And once again, she assured me that everything was going to be all right—and reminded me of all the things I've already accomplished.

My mother and Nia are probably the two people at the heart of my inner circle. They are the people I search for in the stands after a victory. They know me better than anyone. They've seen me at my best, and they've guided me through my worst.

///////

My inner circle includes different kinds of relationships. First and most crucial is my support network. Those are family members, like Nia and my mother—and also my closest friends, people who have been there from the start.

We all need a solid support system in our corner—the kind of people who genuinely care about us and aren't afraid to tell us what we need to hear.

That kind of advice and support is what drowns out the outside noise, which only distracts you from your goals.

The people in my corner keep focused on that pursuit and remind me why I run at all. I intentionally surrounded myself with people who are experts in their fields, knowing they will give me sound advice on the big decisions I need to make. The coaches and trainers I work with are an irreplaceable part of my support system. I need to work with people I trust—people who genuinely want to see me succeed and who have a clear plan for how to help me do that.

In my experience, the best coaches and trainers are the ones who have made mistakes with athletes in the past and have learned from those situations. They are able to adapt and apply those lessons as they move forward. They're experienced enough to fix things when they aren't working.

In sprinting, the smallest injury or mechanical mistake can throw you off. You're dealing with a matter of inches and milliseconds in each race. Your body has to be a fine-tuned machine. You can believe all you want about what you can achieve, but if you haven't prepared your body to actually perform to its best ability, you'll never see the results. A good coach knows how to fine-tune things so that you do. They've been there before—so you can trust that they know exactly what changes to make.

When I first started running with Tony Sharpe, he introduced me to Alban Merepeza.

He was the first chiropractor I worked with. He taught me the mechanics of my body and how to care for it like a finely tuned machine. Running fast is important, he told me, but what you do afterwards is just as critical. He taught me that I needed to be proactive in caring for my body, anticipating issues before they arrived instead of reacting after it was too late.

Alban also became a trusted mentor to me beyond track. As a father in his fifties, he carried a lot of wisdom. And as young man in a fast world, I appreciated his guidance and support. He travelled with me to the Beijing World Championships and the Rio Olympics. After I went pro, he joined me on several Diamond League tours and made the trip south to take care of me. Whenever I was back in Toronto, I'd make the trip out to his clinic in Port Hope or he'd come out to see me at Tony's track in Pickering. Today I still visit with him and his family whenever I get the chance.

When you find people you trust, hang on to them. People like Tony and Alban will always be part of my life because they were so integral to guiding me through the early part of my journey. They continue to be voices I trust.

Surround yourself with people you admire and find inspiration in. People who understand your journey and can offer perspectives that you might not be able to see.

For me, I think of guys like Anson Henry, a mentor who is able to walk me through the challenges that only someone who has been there before can understand. And I think of my first coach, Tony Sharpe, and the constant positive impact he has had on my life. I've always had such respect for Tony because he's an uplifting force in so many people's lives, especially mine.

When I doubted whether I'd be able to return from my hamstring injury, Tony was right there in my ear again. He'd remind me of how far I'd come since we'd first met.

"You're a young man," he'd say. "You've only been doing this for a while. And you came into the sport late. You've got time."

Every conversation we had gave me hope, as though I was still that kid just learning how to sprint, being told I could achieve what seemed impossible.

"You're so wrong," Tony would tell me. "Trust me. You're still learning as you go. You're going to be so much better."

After that, I ended up running a personal best and broke the national record. It was crazy. I remember thinking, "Wow, this guy was actually right."

Your support system also acts like an outside conscience. Kind of like a parent. For me, it means they remind me to stay on top of my nutrition and my hydration. Even though I'm a grown man, I admit that my mom still loves to play that role. She's still always trying to cook me food. She's telling me to eat this and eat that—all things that are healthy and good for you.

I have friends I can talk to about anything. The guys I've known since we were kids, goofing around, who today will get on my case when we're hanging out too late because I have to get to bed. I'll tell them I want to go and party and they'll be like, "Nah, man, you can't do that. You can't come out with us. You have to train tomorrow morning. You need to be locked in."

Find yourself the kind of friends who make you go to bed early instead of hanging out with them. Annoying as it might be, they're the friends who have your best interests at heart. They are the people who hold you accountable, who make sure you're not making bad decisions.

Everyone in my inner circle has, in some way, played a role in my success. Even if it's just a small role, inspiring me through something they've said or been through. They tell me to look at the bright side: Look at what you've accomplished. This is not your defining moment. This is not what's going to define you. You are going to bounce back and you will be better than ever. I think when they remind me of that, it motivates me to get off the couch, to stop moping and being depressed, and to go back out there and show the world who I am.

Your support system should only include people who have a positive influence on you. The kind of people who don't bring negativity with them. There is enough of that everywhere else. These should be people who genuinely want to see you succeed. They want to see you grow, and they take joy in being part of that journey. Those family members who always pump you up. Those friends who want to see you get back on top when you're down. Who remind you of your goals when they see you wandering off course.

Even though I look back at the 2022 season as one filled with obstacles and disappointment, there were still moments of great pride.

Despite a poor performance in the 100 metres and my decision to skip the 200 at the World Championships in Oregon, I managed to win a gold medal alongside my Canadian teammates in the 4 x 100-metre relay. Our victory seemed to shock everyone—but we knew what we were capable of. And despite the doubt and frustration, I believed I could find a way to perform at my best with a medal on the line.

In the end, I took a lot from the season that followed my Olympic gold medal. I had to figure out what went wrong. I had to step back and try to figure out what I could do to make sure it didn't happen again.

But I can't control everything. I need to accept that. I have to remember to keep praying and have faith that things are going to turn around. I believe that what's meant for you is what's meant for you. For me, success in the summer of 2022 wasn't meant to be. I can live with that. You can't control all of the variables. At the end of the day, all you can do is try—and try your absolute best. I've learned how to be satisfied with that.

Sometimes you forget you've accomplished anything at all. Because I'm literally trying to keep building, to keep going. To stay on the podium at the next meet, the next World Championships, the next Olympics. You keep looking ahead, trying to build your legacy as one of the fastest ever.

That's always on my mind. But sometimes you have to *relax*.

It's hard to be content with where you are. There is a balance every person must find, between striving for more and being content with what you've achieved. If you lean too far one way, you risk setting yourself up for failure. You can't relax too much—you can't ignore that natural drive that keeps you pushing. But if you don't take solace in what you've already accomplished, you end up being obsessed with the idea of failure.

By the end of the summer of 2022, everyone in my inner circle was trying to get me to do that. They wanted me to take a vacation—to get away, recharge, and refresh. It was exactly what I needed.

We spend so much time thinking about the next steps. We get so focused on trying to achieve the next big thing that we can forget the achievements that got us to where we are.

Remember that everything takes time. Everything takes patience. That's a message I'm constantly telling my kids now. Like most kids, they want everything *immediately*. I let them know they've got to work for it. You can't just get what you want right away.

And you need to keep telling yourself that even if you take an *L,* it's not really a loss. It's a lesson. A lesson learned. And then you come back—and you win.

I'm not going to just make it back. I'm going to return stronger than I've ever been before. I'm not just saying it: I believe it. I have to.

Because I believe in purpose. I believe things are going to work out. Whatever the outcome is, whether it's what I hope for or something else entirely, in the end, it will work out the way it needs to.

Still, we all get caught up in moments where fear and doubt

creep in. That's inevitable. We psych ourselves out. But you need to continue to be confident and have faith that things are going to work out for the best. Faith in the support and guidance around you.

When you have solid people on your team, it becomes easier to drown out that fear and doubt. It becomes easier to find the motivation to do what you need to do to succeed and believe that you can.

So much about performing your best comes down to *trust*. And when you can trust in the people around you, it becomes that much easier to trust in yourself.

25

TAKE CARE OF YOUR MACHINE

When I was in college, I ate it all.

You name it: Chick-fil-A . . . McDonald's . . . Wendy's . . . Taco Bell.

Whatever was around at the time. Even though I was an elite athlete, I didn't take care of my nutrition at all.

I'm sure I could come up with many reasons for that, but I think the main ones are quite common: I was young, and I had a great metabolism. When I was 20 years old, it didn't seem to matter what I put in my body because I was burning so much energy and the negative effects of the junk I was eating weren't apparent to me.

When I was at USC, we would do body fat testing, but I didn't think much about the results. Coach Caryl told me I was good— and that was good enough for me. I didn't give it a second thought.

My mother was the first one to give me a lecture about my eating habits. This was long before I had kids and a girlfriend, so

I was living on my own. She'd scold me for always eating out and not cooking good things for myself. Whenever she visited, she would cook and make sure that every ingredient was as healthy as possible.

"You've got to start eating better," Mom said. "You've got to put good things in your body."

Of course, she was right. Today, when I look at the success I've had in my career, I believe I owe a lot of it to a conscious effort that I started several years ago to make better decisions about my nutrition and general well-being.

In 2018, after injuring my hamstring for the second time and missing so much competition, I realized I had to change my mentality. I couldn't play around anymore. It was all different now. There was too much on the line, and I knew how vulnerable I was to breaking down if I didn't take proper care of my health.

Injuries like that don't just happen on the track in the heat of performance. I might have torn my hamstring at that moment, but I'd unknowingly set myself up for that injury long before. As I recovered, many people encouraged me to start taking the necessary steps in other areas if I wanted to keep pushing the boundaries of my ability.

I remember going through all the protocols to determine that my hamstring was healed. I had MRIs, X-rays, and ultrasounds to tell me everything was finally fine. But as an elite athlete, fine isn't good enough. Though my hamstring was okay in relation to a regular person, I was still a long way from being in a position where I could be confident I wouldn't reinjure it while running at high speed and intensity. If I was going to get back to where I wanted to be, I needed to be much more mindful about how to get there. The specialist I was seeing at the time recommended that I consult a nutritionist.

A blood test revealed I had low vitamin D and I needed to get more iron. My vitamin C levels were also down, and my immune system was compromised. At the time, I had no idea that a weakened immune system could cause fatigue. Or that my diet had a direct effect on inflammation in my body. Through discussions with my nutritionist and hours spent researching on Google, I started to understand that what I put in my body had greater importance than I'd ever considered. It had a clear effect on my ability to perform and how susceptible I was to injury.

Even though I'd already had success on the track, this was the first time I started to think deeply about areas I'd been blind to in my younger days.

Maybe I need to do better with my nutrition, I realized. Maybe I need to do better with my hydration and replenishing electrolytes. Maybe I need to be more focused on rest and recovery. This was about planning to be the best and understanding that real preparation considers every aspect that influences my performance.

Today, I eat quinoa. I *never* used to eat quinoa before.

I also have an Olympic gold medal. I'd never had one of those before either.

This isn't a plug for an "Andre De Grasse Quinoa-Only Nutrition Plan," but it is a challenge to anyone reading this book to adopt healthy common-sense habits when it comes to what you decide to put into your body. Over the past few years, I've learned just how critical those habits are when it comes to reaching your potential and achieving your goals.

In the simplest of terms, what I learned after my prolonged

absence because of injuries was that I needed to clean up my diet. Even though my hamstring was healed, I had to focus on other areas I'd been missing out on to help me accomplish my goals. The last thing I wanted was to end up injured again.

My two main areas of concern were inflammation and fatigue. Both of those issues were contributing to my injuries, so I had to make sure that anything I put into my body wasn't contributing to either of those problems.

It wasn't complicated. There wasn't any special formula or program for me to follow. It was really all about being smart and eating smart. My nutritionist outlined the kinds of foods I should focus on eating, and my own inclination to research helped fill in all the specifics. We have so much knowledge at our fingertips today, there isn't any excuse to not be able to educate yourself through credible resources.

Specifically, I focused on eating more vegetables and other foods that help keep your energy high. I also tried to get as much vitamin C as possible, to keep my immune system firing. Before taking that blood test and consulting an expert, I had no idea my vitamin C levels were down and my immune system was compromised. Travelling all the time put me in a particularly vulnerable position. It's one thing to be training in the same place every day and then heading home. But flying from continent to continent, city to city, meeting hundreds of people, makes me much more susceptible to viruses. Even if I wasn't getting sick, my weakened immune system was causing me to have lower energy levels.

Even when I'm at the Olympics or a World Championships, I just try to use my head and be sensible about what I eat. I stay away from fried food and raw food. I make sure that everything is grilled. There are different selections when you go to the cafeteria at an event like the Olympics, and as you can imagine they are all pretty healthy. But even then, you need to be careful. For example, I make sure I don't overeat. I focus on consuming good carbs and vegetables. If there's chicken, which is great, I make sure it's as plain as possible. Chill on the sauce! Just stay away from the extras.

The other area I had to consider was body fat. Some people will be surprised by how much a sprinter like me must pay attention to their body fat percentage, given how fit we have to be just to reach that level. But I need to keep my body fat under a certain percentage to know I'm in an optimal position to compete. The smallest change can have an impact on performance and the susceptibility to injury. Sometimes I need to lose weight. When you run with too much body fat it can lead to injuries. But sometimes I need to gain weight, adding muscle. Our bodies are constantly changing, so this is one of the areas I pay the most attention to.

Every fall I take about a month off from training, just to give myself a mental and physical break from the grind of constantly training and racing. When I get back to it, my body fat has increased a touch. This year it was about 7 percent, so I had to work to get it back down to around 5 percent. If I can get it there by the time competitions start up again, I know I'll be in good shape.

As a sprinter, my body is a different machine than what my competitors are working with. It just depends on the person. It depends on your body type. It depends on your height and how much you weigh. For me, my approach fluctuates every single year because my weight fluctuates a lot, which is normal for most people.

I've gotten heavier as I've gotten older. When I first started, I weighed about 140 pounds—but now I'm consistently around 160 pounds. I've put on 20 to 25 pounds in a span of eight or nine years. Part of that gain was just natural, adding strength with age. Part of it was deliberate. As I've aged, I've focused on adding power in my stride through increased muscle mass.

Age changes everything, doesn't it?

I'm not old, by normal standards. But as an elite athlete, I'm so in tune with how my body feels that every minor change has an impact. When I was just starting out, there were very few changes that affected me. I could recover quickly. But as I've gotten older, each year has made a difference. You start to feel it more.

Before, when I'd run six races during competition (between the 100 and 200 metres), I felt good. I was like, "Now I'm ready for the relay!"

As I got older, I'd run six races doing the 100 and 200 and be like, "Damn, my legs are dead. I have to try to muscle out this relay now."

It was just different. My body was getting older. It wasn't recovering as fast as it did when I was 20 or 21 years old. The machine needed to be monitored much more than it used to.

That meant I had to make sure I was on top of my health in ways I just hadn't been before.

When I started to pay close attention to my nutrition back in 2018, I became much more aware of how the small, everyday decisions I made about my body and how I treat it directly affected my performance. My nutrition was central to that process. What I put into my body not only fuelled the effectiveness of my workout but also affected my recovery.

If I'm putting junk into my body, I feel like junk the next day. I feel slow and sluggish. I can tell that my body hasn't recovered from my previous workout the way it needs to, and that my energy levels are way down.

I went from eating what I want to being as conscious about my diet as I am about my training. And I felt the change very quickly.

At the time my training regimen had switched from going four days a week to hitting the track six days a week. It was a way bigger load on my body. But with a better diet, I found I was able to get more out of my practices. I was able to get through more reps. I had more energy throughout each session. My body didn't break down as easily after a couple of days of training.

Hydration is another key aspect of my health that I've learned to be conscious about. It's a vital thing that people always seem to forget. And it's the easiest. Drink water. Drink water constantly.

It's especially key for me when I'm training out in the sun for two or three hours. I drink a lot while I'm on the track, but it's the hours afterwards when it's most critical that I drink as much water as possible. If I'm dehydrated on the track, my muscles are going to start to fatigue. I also drink a lot of Gatorade to replenish electrolytes in my system, which help with hydration and also regulate nerve and muscle function.

If you're not an elite athlete, you might not notice it as much. But for an elite athlete it's kind of like your butter. It can be the difference between tweaking or tearing a muscle. I'm also fortunate because Athletics Canada and Gatorade both provide sweat tests to monitor levels of hydration, so they help me see how my hydration is coming throughout the season.

A regular person probably won't think that much about it

because they're not performing a high-intensity activity, but it still affects how you feel. Be cognizant of what you're lacking, especially when life gets busy.

I don't have a set target for the amount of water I drink in a day—though you can easily find the recommended amount for your own body type and needs. The most common guideline seems to be eight 8-ounce glasses for an adult. For me, though, it's more of a common-sense approach. I just drink. If I don't need to go to the bathroom regularly, that means I'm not drinking enough. Or if your urine isn't clear enough, you need to down some more H_2O. After making regular hydration a habit, I'm also much more aware of how my body feels. I can just tell when I'm getting a little bit dehydrated.

When I get close to a competition, I'm a little more conscious about it—as I am with all aspects of my training and nutrition. But again, it doesn't have to be that complicated. These are simple habits that can help you unlock the energy and wellness you need in order to reach your peak potential every day.

Finally, always remember that sleep is number one. It's probably the most critical element of all the areas I need to take care of to perform my best. Forget everything else. If you're not getting sleep, then it's just over.

In my world if you don't get sleep the consequences are obvious. You're not going to run fast. You're going to get injured. Again, though, this is just common sense. If you don't get sleep, you're going to be a zombie. You don't need any in-depth studies to tell you that. We've all felt what being a zombie is like at some point in our lives.

I try to get eight hours of sleep a night. I usually get to bed between 10 and 10:30 at night. I'm a pretty good sleeper, so I usually sleep through the night—unless I have to get out of bed to pee, which just means I'm hydrating properly.

You can get away with poor nutrition a little bit, but you can't get away with not getting enough sleep. That's the Grim Reaper.

My focus on nutrition, hydration, and sleep unlocked another level in my performance. I believe they were the key habits that led to my successful return from injury and ultimately to gold in Tokyo. And I believe that making small changes in your daily approach to these key areas can unlock so much potential for you too.

But how do you balance it all?

Make those areas a priority, and then they become part of your lifestyle.

That takes discipline and practice. I keep saying our approach doesn't need to be complicated, but that doesn't mean it's easy. Life is busy. It's hard and it's stressful. And when we feel the most overwhelmed, we often lose sight of the simple habits that keep us moving effectively.

Today, keeping on top of my nutrition, hydration, and sleep is harder than ever. I need to find a balance between training, my sponsor responsibilities, and being a parent and partner. Preparing quality food takes time, and there is only so much time in a day.

It's amazing how even the smallest things eat into that time, isn't it? We recently moved from Jacksonville to Orlando, and right away it was apparent just how much more time we were spending in the car in Orlando, where everything seems much more spread out. Traffic eats up time too!

Still, we don't overprepare.

We don't plan out our meals for the week and stick to a specific plan. Because in real life—the life of a parent with several young kids—those plans almost always go off the rails. Instead, we make a conscious effort to bring only healthy food into our house and to make sure that even if we need to pull something together at the last minute, it's going to be something healthy. We focus on having protein in our freezer—lean meat, like chicken—and lots of vegetables on hand. We cut out the chips and cookies. That can be a challenge with kids in the house. Of course, we have some fun food for them. But where I used to sneak a handful of animal crackers, I avoid the kids' snacks altogether.

Nia and I are on the move a lot. If one of us is returning from competition in a different time zone, then we prioritize helping them get the rest they need to be back on track. Sometimes that means taking the kids for the afternoon so the other person can get in a long nap. Or maybe it's as easy as one of us picking up the kids from school so the other can get an extra half-hour of rest. Because we both operate in the same world as track athletes, training side by side, we are aligned in what we both need to perform our best as people, as parents, and as athletes.

Today, for me, this holistic approach is all part of a game plan laid out by my team: my coach, my nutritionist, my trainer. Everybody must be on the same page, working towards the same common target. I don't overthink it. I follow the plan. And I make my nutrition, hydration, and sleep a central priority so I can perform my best.

Please remember that everyone is different. We are not operating under the same pressures or with the same opportunities.

First of all, most people don't have an entire team of professionals to keep them on track. And my nutritional needs as an elite athlete are likely not the same as yours. And it's unlikely you'll see the negative impact of being lax in these areas the way I do, because your performance isn't being measured in fractions of a second each day (unless you're also training as a sprinter full time, six days a week).

In a busy life, these areas are so easy to forget about. That's why you need to be deliberate and stubborn about making diet, hydration, and sleep an immovable priority. Make them unbreakable habits. Don't relent.

That's also why I think it's helpful for everyone to take the time to see a nutritionist and get professional advice that is specific to your needs. You owe that to yourself.

Have your blood tested to find out where your deficiencies are. Every piece of information you can get about your body will help you understand it more. Know what is working in your body and what is lacking. Find out where you're deficient and address it. Find the balance. If you have high cholesterol, you've got to chill on the foods that cause it. Eat those greens.

Remember that regardless of whether you're an elite athlete or just someone trying to unlock more energy to be their best each day, the process doesn't need to feel like you're solving a puzzle. Don't overthink it. It's common sense. Make these healthy choices a daily habit. Let those healthy habits give you the strength and energy to be your best.

26

BEYOND GOLD

There is a lot of noise out there. I probably don't have to tell you that. If you spend any time on social media, you know it very well.

It happens in every sport—and really every walk of life. Whether you let that control you or not is up to you. That noise can get in your head if you let it. It combines with self-doubt that you already feel and compounds it.

I do my best to avoid it. I'm better at staying away from social media today than I was several years ago, but my friends still let me know when someone is slamming me on Twitter or Instagram. They tell me I need to go prove so-and-so wrong: "They're talking shit about you, man! Prove them wrong!"

I always get a laugh out of that.

Your friends are always good at reminding you there are people out there taking shots at you. But I'm not worried about what haters think about my ability. I've had plenty of them in my life so far and I've proven enough of them wrong to know they don't have any power over me. You can't let it eat you up inside.

There is also a positive side to social media. For as much trolling as you might face, there are people who take time to let you know that what you've done has been an inspiration to them. There are people who take the time to let you know you helped get them through a difficult time, just by seeing you run a race. That means a lot. For any negative feelings that might come when people try to tear you down, hearing you have been an inspiration to even a single person makes it all worthwhile.

I think it's key to not get too caught up in the negative or the positive. To do that, I've learned it's essential to keep a balanced perspective on life.

I find that taking time to connect with friends and family has been the biggest help in this area. The people who know me best are the most capable of knowing when I'm going through a hard time. They also understand me well enough that they know exactly what I need to hear, when I need to hear it. Chatting with my closest friends also keeps me grounded. I try to find out what's going on in their lives. We vent together, as good friends always do. It reminds me of how small my problems actually are, when you put them in perspective. If I am concerned about losing a race, it's not the same thing as a good friend of mine losing their job. The world I grew up in is filled with *real* challenges, problems, and stress.

Anyone who has been able to make a substantial living competing in a sport should be humble enough to realize they live a blessed life. I've been given a remarkable opportunity in life, and I have a responsibility to make the most of it. Whenever I start to feel bad about something I am going through on the track, I lean on my family and friends to help me keep it all in perspective. I'm going to be all right.

Whenever I'm feeling down about a performance, I try to zoom out. I remind myself that I've made it all the way to the top. I've accomplished so much just to get here. No matter what happens, I have a lot to be proud of and a lot to be grateful for. The fact that I have anything to be down about at all is an accomplishment.

Of course, you don't need to be an Olympic champion to find joy and perspective in your accomplishments. This is something everyone can and should do. When I speak with my friends who are going through a rough patch, I try to give them that advice as well. Whatever they're doing in their careers, I remind them to think about how far they've come from where we all started. Reminiscing about the past can be a great way to keep the present in perspective. Not that long ago we were just kids, goofing around and dreaming of what we might become one day. Recently I was chatting with one of my friends who started his own HVAC and air conditioning company. He's worked so hard to get it off the ground. And he loves the work he does. He's been successful enough to buy his own truck. The other week he bought a Mercedes-Benz. I was so happy to see all the sweat he's put into building his company pay off the way it has. Another friend of mine recently launched his own clothing line called Spiritual Army and is doing serious numbers! And one of the guys I loved playing basketball with is now coaching the game at a high level. I love hearing about my friends' successes.

Our paths are all different, but our accomplishments are all significant. I don't think people give themselves enough credit for what they've achieved. Pause for a moment to look at how far *you've* come in life. Think of all the things you've accomplished. Give yourself credit for that. We all work hard to overcome unique obstacles. We all deal with different challenges. One of the keys to being able to push through the next hard thing we do is to be proud of all the hard things we've overcome before.

It takes baby steps, sometimes. There are going to be more disappointments in life. There are going to be challenges that we fail. But those will only defeat you if you let them. You just need to keep going. "Life is full of wins and losses, baby," as I always like to say.

For me, it took me a while to become an Olympic champion. I wanted to win a gold medal in Rio, even though others probably didn't expect it of me. While I was proud of the medals I did win, my goal was still gold. It took a long time for me to be able to get a second chance. So much happens in the four years between Olympic Games for an athlete. And when the wait is extended by a global pandemic, the wait gets even longer. For five years, since Rio, I wondered if I would ever achieve my dream of becoming an Olympic champion. At times, that dream seemed very far away. I had to battle through World Championships and the disappointment that followed when I didn't walk away with the results I wanted.

Sometimes I'd wonder, "Am I ever going to be a world champion? Am I ever going to be an Olympic champion? Will I ever get to hang a gold medal around my neck?"

When I felt that doubt rising, I had to push it away by reminding myself that, no matter what happens, I've already achieved more than I dreamed of. As much as I want to win—as much as I wanted that gold medal dream to come true—if I couldn't quite get there, I'd still have so much to be proud of. When you realize you can lift the weight of a moment off your shoulders, you become lighter and freer to perform the way you know you can. The gravity of expectation and doubt can be conquered.

Maybe I'm able to relax a bit more than some of my competitors because track wasn't what I wanted to do my whole life. I've seen a lot of people struggle in my sport because sprinting is all they know. It's all they've ever done. The expectation they put on themselves is enormous. It's a heavy weight to carry. They can't imagine a world in which they aren't an elite sprinter or an elite athlete. If you step back you can see how easily that translates to other professions. There are people who can't imagine their lives if they weren't an elite doctor, lawyer, or CEO. There are people who wrap up their identities in achievements and careers. I'm not sure whether that's a mistake or not. It could be a good thing or a bad thing—I'm not sure.

I always try to remind myself that there is something else I could be doing—something that might bring me as much joy as sprinting does. There will always be something else I want to accomplish. Whatever happens with track is just icing on the cake for me now that I've accomplished my dream of becoming an Olympic champion. In the future, I'll be able to find something else I want to do just as much. I can only do this job for a limited amount of time in my life, so I don't want to get caught up in the stress of it. I need to enjoy every moment and do the best I can.

That doesn't mean I don't believe in working hard to reach your goals. That's what drives me. But it does mean keeping everything in proper perspective and reminding yourself that you are much more than what you do—and your value is worth much more than the gold medals around your neck, the achievements on your resume, or the money in your bank account.

Never define yourself by what you have achieved or by what you are yet to achieve. Instead, be proud of what you've done to stand where you do—and remember how far you've come to get there.

27

FAMILY FIRST

My kids changed my life completely.

Our first child, Yuri, was born in Philadelphia, where Nia grew up and her parents still live. That's what she considers home.

I was in Philly leading up to Yuri's birth in June 2018. Suddenly, I was a dad. Obviously, I knew the baby was coming, but I still felt like I was in complete shock as I held her little body in my arms. It took me a while to hold her. I was so nervous because she came out so small. She was four pounds and 12 ounces. So she was tiny (especially compared with my son, who was way bigger, about seven pounds, when he was born three years later).

Neither of us wanted to know the sex before the baby was born, so it was all a surprise. I was looking for the penis and I didn't see anything, and then everyone was like, "It's a girl." And I was kind of taken aback. I was like, "I have a daughter. Wow."

It was all so different for me. Just a new type of feeling, something I'd never experienced before.

"Okay, I'm a dad," I thought. "I guess I have to do things differently now."

Life is going to change. Things are evolving. I've got to pick up this parenting thing quickly.

And yes, everything changed—*fast*.

I had to leave for a couple days after she was born to run in the Harry Jerome Track Classic in Vancouver. I was operating on no sleep, but I'd committed to running the 100 and 4 x 100. That was the first time I realized just how exhausting it is to be a parent!

After sleep-running through the meet, I returned to Philadelphia and we stayed for a couple of weeks, getting settled into our new world. Nia and I got Yuri a passport and they came to Toronto to stay with me while I continued my rehab and the long process to get back to top form.

My schedule was relatively easy, as I tried to slow down and take it all in. It wasn't crazy like it is now. But it sure felt crazy! The baby was crying every two seconds. In the middle of night! We'd get up and try to settle her down. I was like, "Oh my gosh, I want to sleep!"

I can *still* hear the baby crying!

It was so different. I remember thinking, "What just happened? What did I sign up for?"

This is a whole new job in itself.

But the crazy part was how much I loved it.

We live in Florida now. Nia and I both trained in Jacksonville before we moved to the Orlando area. It's pretty cool. We live near lakes that have alligators swimming by and giant frogs hopping around. Some deer live in the neighbourhood as well. It's a fun place to raise a family.

I usually train from about 10 a.m. to 3 p.m., between time spent on the track and in the gym. Nia is usually on a similar schedule with her training. It's a full day. We get home around 4 p.m. That's when the kids take over. We're going full out in parent mode until about 8 p.m., if we're lucky. They are energetic kids. We go to bed exhausted, and then we get up the next day and do it all again.

On the odd occasion that no one is around when I get home, I usually try to sleep.

Those naps when you're totally exhausted just feel so good.

It's a tiring life.

But I love it. I wouldn't trade any of it for the world. I'd give up my Olympic medals if it meant I could spend each day with my kids.

The reality, though, is that I need to spend a lot of time away because of my profession. I attend around a dozen meets each season, which takes me all over the world. I might be in Rome one weekend, Monaco the next, and then in Asia or Africa the week after. Nia is often in different places. We have great support for the kids between our families. But it takes a toll. We're lucky to do what we love and to see the world doing it. But that doesn't make it easy. And it's even harder when you have young kids—you miss them and they miss you. We spend a lot of hours on FaceTime, oceans apart.

Life on the circuit is difficult for a young family. But there are all kinds of families who deal with unique challenges. Sometimes it's easy to lose sight of the most important things in life when you are busy trying to pursue your goals and achieve difficult things.

Pause whenever you can to remember why you do what you do. At the end of the day, what's the most indispensable thing to you? What part of your world could you not live without?

For me, that's family.

They are the centre of everything I do. At this point in my life and my career, I understand that more than anything. I find motivation and inspiration in my kids and in my partner, Nia. We've built an incredible life together. Everything I do is for them.

When I think about what I set out to achieve in my career, I now think about what will make my family proud of me. Not only when it comes to the medals I win but to the type of life I can provide for them as well. And the kind of father they see me as.

I want to be a good role model for my kids, making sure I set a strong foundation for them. That's what keeps me going.

I think part of the reason I'm so determined to be close with my kids is because of the relationship I had with my own father.

I haven't shared much about my father before. I usually don't want to bring it up in media interviews, because it's difficult for other people to convey how I feel about my father. I don't want anyone else to twist my words. So I usually just don't go there. It's easier that way.

But I've been thinking about him a lot lately.

My father, Alex Waithe, was very sick in December 2020, battling stage-four pancreatic cancer.

My older sister, who was close with him, messaged me to let me know it wasn't looking good and that he would likely pass away soon.

"This is happening," she told me. "I think you should come home and see him."

But in the days before his death, I didn't make the trip to visit him. He died on January 31, 2021. He was 64 years old.

My father was born in Barbados and came to Canada alone when he was 15 years old to go to school. He and my mother met in Toronto when she was in her mid-20s.

Dad wasn't around very often when I was young, but as a kid you don't know any better. At the time, it was Mom and me. She was my world, and that was enough. I saw how hard she worked and would learn to appreciate that as I got older. She is always there for me, through everything. Somehow, she never missed a game and rarely missed a practice.

Maybe because Mom was always there, that became all I needed when I was young. Maybe that was all either of us really needed.

As you get older, you start to realize you're missing something. Not love or support—my mother provided more of that than any kid could need. But it was the awareness of an absence. You meet other kids and learn about their families. And you start to wonder why your father isn't around. Why does this figure that other kids have in their lives not exist in yours?

I was probably in the sixth grade, when I was about 10 or 11, when I first got to know my father. We started hanging out regularly on the weekends. He'd pick me up on Saturdays, always in a different rental car that smelled fresh and new. We'd go to the movies a lot, and he'd take me to his favourite go-to restaurants, Red Lobster and Swiss Chalet. We'd play a card game called rummy. And we'd play checkers. He taught me how to play dominoes. It was cool, playing all these little games with him. Hanging out with him was always fun.

It was nice to get to know my father during those weekends

together, but it wasn't an everyday type of thing. He rented a small apartment in the Davisville area of Toronto, but I never visited him there.

I enjoyed spending time with my father. He was a fun, charismatic guy. And he was also smart and engaging.

My father was a high school counsellor and night school principal in Toronto. He retired in his late 50s, when I was still a kid. He lived in the GTA part of the time, but he'd always go back home to Barbados. He spent most of his time there. Usually he was in Toronto during the summers when I was out of school. Before he met my mother, he had a couple of other kids from a previous marriage. They were about a decade older than me. I didn't even know I had a brother and sister until I was eight or nine years old.

That was quite a surprise, but I loved it. Suddenly I had two older siblings to look up to, even if they were complete strangers when we met. They'd both become role models in my life, so that was a real blessing.

I saw my father most summer weekends through my teenage years. I even went to Barbados to visit him, along with my three siblings, Alexandra, Julian, and Dantee. He took me to the beach. He'd introduce me to his friends and we'd go to parties, because in the islands you can start partying and drinking when you're much younger than you can in Canada. He'd ask if I wanted a beer. It was fun. He knew I was responsible.

Everyone seemed to love my father. He was a radio host and often a DJ and MC at parties and celebrations in Barbados. I love music, I love to dance, and my father is probably where I got a little bit of that. He was into all that kind of stuff. He'd take me to the record store and I would get CDs of artists he enjoyed from genres he introduced me to, like jazz, calypso, and reggae. He also had great recommendations for hip hop and R&B.

My father used to play cricket in Barbados. When I went to visit him, he took me to the cricket pitch and showed me how to play. It was the first time I ever played. It's the only real sports memory that we shared. It's one of my favourite memories from my teenage years.

I admired my father. He was cool. But he had a lot going on; he was always on the go. Still, he was a good man. Everyone who knew him spoke so highly of him. I like to think I carry on some of his traits in the way I interact with people. My mom is quiet and reserved, but my dad was so outgoing. I definitely have both characteristics, and I think the moments when I'm able to engage with people and break away from my introverted side are a gift from him.

I never asked my mom about the details of what happened with them or why Dad wasn't a bigger, more constant part of my life. Maybe I never really wanted to find out the answers. Maybe I'd find out one day; or maybe I wouldn't. Either way, I just left it alone when I was growing up.

I've been asked if it was tough sometimes as a kid to not have him around. Did I wish my dad could have been there to watch me play sports? When I was winning the provincials in baseball? When I was playing AAU basketball? When I first started running track?

I don't know.

As I got older I actually had a lot of friends who didn't grow up with their dad as well. So I wasn't the only one going through that type of stuff. I thought about it more but didn't dwell on it. I didn't want it to get to me. I had to keep moving forward. I started building my own life, moving towards my own goals and dreams. And things worked out.

I knew my father was there. I knew anytime I wanted to talk to him, I could. I just never chose to do that.

I do have regrets, of course. When I reached the level I did as a runner—travelling the world, sprinting alongside and beating the fastest men alive—I didn't get a chance to share that with my father. He watched me compete at the Pan Am Games in Toronto, and he came to the Rio Olympics. He was in the stadium when I won each of those medals and, really, emerged for the first time on the global stage. The Rio stands were really high up, but I found him among the mass of people and managed to share that moment with him, even though it was all a blur. I didn't leave the Olympic Village much, so I wasn't able to celebrate with him there.

I don't blame my father or have any ill will or resentment towards him. The relationship I had with him just wasn't as close as the one I have with my mom.

Of course, there are questions I wish I still had the time to ask him. There are lessons I'd love to be able to learn from him. I wish my father was still alive.

I wish he'd been able to see his son win that gold medal in Tokyo.

I wish he'd been able to see the kind of father I've become. I think he'd be proud of all that. Maybe down the road we might have grown closer. I'd love to have shared one more beer with him, learning more about the music he loved.

But I'm not angry we weren't closer when I was growing up—or that we never had the chance to connect as men.

"It is what it is," as people say. And I think I understand what that means more than most.

I don't even know what I was going through in my mind before my father died.

My father battled prostate cancer for years without telling anyone. But then he got sick from COVID while he was in Barbados, and it nearly killed him. When he got a little bit better for a time, he returned to Canada to seek medical treatment. But his health started to decline again and he ended up back in hospital.

We were living in Florida and were still dealing with the restrictions of the pandemic. My father was in the hospital in Toronto, and there were all sorts of strict protocols for entering Canada. That was part of it. But I was also preparing for the Tokyo Olympics at the time. And Nia was pregnant with our second child. I had my own family to worry about. I couldn't just get up and leave them. Anyone with young kids can appreciate the responsibility. Yuri was a toddler and my stepson Titus was just starting school—and another kid was on the way. Our son was due in May.

So I just didn't go. It wasn't something I wanted to get emotional about. I just kind of left it alone and hoped he was going to make it.

But he didn't.

I hadn't lost any family before. But I've lost friends. One of my good friends from the ninth grade died of a seizure while playing video games. That's a tough thing to process when you're a kid, and I probably never did.

I've never lost someone I'm truly close to before.

I'm still processing my father's death. There were a lot of questions I wanted to ask him. Like why weren't you around more? Why weren't we closer when I was younger? I didn't get to have that conversation with him. It never came up when I was younger, and we didn't have the chance to talk about it when I was older. But maybe that was because I was too scared to know the answer. Or maybe I already knew the reason in the back of my mind. It happens all the time with kids, so my situation wasn't anything special.

It is what it is, right?

That's why I've always told myself that whatever happens in my life, I'll make sure I'm always in my kids' lives.

My experience with my father shapes the way I am as a dad. I know what kind of father I'm going to be for my kids.

I want to be there all the time—whatever sports they play, whatever hobbies they have. A dance recital, a spelling bee—anything. Whatever they put their mind to, I just want to make sure I'm there for it, above everything else.

Family first. Before everything.

Often when we set out to achieve great things, it's easy to lose sight of what matters. We take the people around us for granted and forget that we don't know how much time we have to share with them. Don't let that happen. Life is never too busy to make space for the people you love. Nothing you accomplish can compare to the happiness that being with those people will give you. As a son, I know what it's like to long for a more intimate and meaningful bond with a parent—and now as a parent, I know the absolute joy that having that kind of connection with a child brings. It doesn't need to be a parent and child connection though. It can be connections to siblings, or cousins, or friends—people you've known for a lifetime or the people you'll meet in years to come. However your family looks, however it's made up, make the people in it the priority of your life. If you do, every other pursuit will carry so much more meaning.

28

COMPARTMENTS

'm often asked how I am able to juggle all the different aspects of my life—from training to competing to public appearances and my charitable and sponsorship commitments, on top of having a young family. (Oh yeah, and writing this book!)

The truth is, like most parents, I don't really know. Sometimes a day will go by and I'll have no idea how we got through it.

People have told me I come across as relaxed and chill. It might seem like there is very little going on in my life to stress me out. But in reality, behind it all, there is a lot happening.

The neat thing about my family is that I get to spend so much time with my partner because we're both elite athletes who train together. When neither of us gets sleep because one of our kids is up through the night, there is no moaning about it at practice the next day. If Nia is working hard, I'm working hard—there are no excuses.

Between both of our careers, we juggle a lot. But we've managed to keep a healthy balance of time and energy management by setting our priorities and compartmentalizing our schedules.

Our goal is to put ourselves in a position to be our best selves in each area of our lives.

We know our limits when it comes to what we can commit to beyond our family. Our first priority is to be the best parents we can be.

The next box is our careers, which means our training takes precedence over other obligations. We need to give ourselves the space to train and to properly rest so we are able to continue to perform at an elite level. That means being strict about what we commit to beyond the track.

Of course, our professional obligations are closely tied to that. As I've said, much of my financial well-being relies on my endorsements and other partnerships off the track. I'm not able to take those relationships and obligations for granted. That means my schedule is often filled with trips for commercial shoots and events. As I've gotten older—and especially as I've become a father—I've learned to be honest about what I am able to take on and to let people know when it's simply too much. If I didn't do that at times, I'd be jeopardizing my commitment to my success on the track and to my family. As important as those off-track commitments are, I need to keep my priorities in order.

At the same time, Nia and I both know we are going to fall short in each of the key areas of our lives at times. Nobody is a perfect parent. Nobody is a perfect athlete. As much as we try to be mindful of the order of our priorities, we're inevitably going to lose sight of them at times. We lean on each other for support, especially in those moments. Because we're so aligned, we can help keep each other focused on our goals and priorities.

I've also found that kids are a constant source of motivation. When I come home from a hard day of training feeling exhausted, I somehow find a burst of energy when the kids want to play. And when I show up at the track feeling beat, I find an extra gear thinking of them watching me run. They're getting to the age now where they won't let us slack off, even if we wanted. They watch our performances and let us know whether they think we did our best or not. When your toddler is telling you that you need to try harder, that's a voice you can't ignore.

With all of the demands I juggle in my career and with my family, I need to be very diligent about staying on top of my schedule. That comes down to compartmentalizing too. Paul Doyle and Robby Hughes, my track agents, manage my competition obligations, setting my schedule for the upcoming season. My marketing agent Brian Levine and his team organize my sponsorship obligations as well as my charity work and the related media interviews I do, making sure those commitments work within my track schedule. My coach lays out when I need to arrive at training each day. I factor in time for rest and physical therapy, with regular massage and chiropractic treatments. When I'm dealing with an injury, as I did through the 2022 season with nagging pain in my toe, treating that becomes the priority.

The simplest trick I've learned for keeping track of it all is to enter everything into my calendar the moment I'm told about it. If I get lazy about doing that, I'm bound to miss a flight or fail to show up for an appearance. It's a small habit, but such a valuable one. Without a constantly updated calendar, I'd be lost.

I'm fortunate to have a great team that keeps me on track. Everyone I work with has my best interests in mind. They know when I'm overwhelmed and need a break. They know when I need to be nudged to get something done. When so much of your life depends on your time and energy, having a great support system around you is key.

One of the key people in that area is Robby. He makes sure I don't get lost in all the chaos. He books my flights and takes care of all my accommodations. He travels with me when I'm on the road. He keeps everything organized and on track. He makes sure I have my spikes and everything I need at a meet. He makes sure I'm eating and preparing properly. When you're dealing with all the demands of a meet while trying to prepare mentally, it's easy to lose sight of the obvious stuff—like eating. Robby keeps me going. It's also just nice to have someone to be with when you're out on a trip away from your family and friends. That can be very lonely. He's a great guy who is fun to chill with. He makes my life a lot easier.

We all live busy lives. We all take on probably more than we should at times. We all get overwhelmed and feel like we can't keep up.

In my experience, the best way to avoid that kind of burn-out is to first be clear about your priorities. Know what matters most to you, and protect the time and energy you spend doing that at all costs. Everything else should fall beneath that, in order of importance. Then allot your time accordingly. Make sure you give yourself the space and rest to be able to be your best self within each of those areas. If you're at home with your family, focus on being the best parent and partner you can be in that moment. If you are in class or studying in the library, shut off all distractions and make the most of that time. At work? Same thing. When you feel like you're not doing your best, step back and figure out why.

In a busy life of striving for success, managing your time and energy is one of the most fundamental tasks—and often the most overlooked. As an athlete, the compartments in my life are so clearly defined that it's perhaps easier for me to identify them. My unique family life, with a partner I also train with, helps keep me focused on track. I know that few people operate within those kinds of circumstances. But if you think about it, you probably have specific areas in your life that you can break into compartments. Set a hierarchy of priorities first, and then set out a schedule that allows you to be your best self in each of those areas. But also keep your focus on your priorities. In your quest for excellence, the order of those compartments should rarely shift.

29

MEDALS TARNISH

I didn't meet my older siblings until I was in middle school, but they quickly became a cherished part of my life.

My sister's name is Alexandra, and she's a decade older than I am. My brother's name is Julian. He's eight years older than me.

Julian was in high school when we met. I thought he was so cool, and I always wanted to hang out with him. I didn't even think of him as a half-brother. Whenever I introduced him to people, I was like, "This is my brother."

I'd always call him and ask him what he was up to.

"Can we hang out?"

And almost always, Julian would say yes. He and my sister lived together near Davisville subway station in Toronto.

He'd arrange to pick me up on the weekend so we could hang out, because he was in school all week. If he couldn't pick me up in Markham, I'd take the subway to go see him.

We'd go to the movies together, we'd play basketball at the rec centre, we'd play Ping-Pong—whatever I wanted to do, Julian was down for. It was just me and him.

I would always hang out with him Friday or Saturday night, then he'd drop me back in Markham after. Or if he wanted to go out Saturday night and didn't want his sixth-grade sibling tagging along, he'd drive me back that afternoon.

I didn't realize at the time, but Julian became a pretty big mentor in my life during that period. I just thought I was hanging out with a cool older brother, but really, he was teaching me valuable life lessons I wouldn't appreciate until I was much older.

Julian encouraged me to keep pursuing sports. I played for two different well-known AAU basketball teams through my teenage years, Triple Bounce and Toronto Missions. Julian encouraged me to use those abilities to try to land a scholarship. It wasn't so much about the sport for him as it was about the opportunity to get a good education. He tried to keep me on the right path, showing me what I could do—rather than telling me what I couldn't. He wanted me to find a passion that would be fulfilling and meaningful as a career.

Julian is street smart. He's passionate about social issues. He cares about people. While completing his degree in social work, he worked in Regent Park, an area in Toronto known for a lot of social housing. He brought me to work with him to show me what it was all about. It was kind of like one of those "take your kid to work" days, but this was more of a "take your little half-brother to work" day.

I was in high school at the time, and I didn't know what I wanted to do after I graduated. I just kind of felt stuck. I remember thinking, "This is not working out." I was worried about my future.

I spent a lot of time with my friends, just chilling and smoking weed. I wasn't on track to do anything exceptional with my life. I was still trying to figure out what my purpose was.

Julian thought I might enjoy working with at-risk youth and others in marginalized communities like Regent Park. He brought me around and introduced me to people, showing me all the stuff he did on a regular basis.

"Some of it's good, some of it's not," he told me. "It can be challenging. But I think you would like it. I think there's a lot you would enjoy doing, because you want to see other kids be successful."

It certainly wasn't glamorous work, but it was work that really mattered. It was clear that Julian was making a difference in people's lives every day. He told me it was the kind of work that has good days and bad days. You take a lot of shit and it could be ugly at times. But when it goes well, he said, you feel good about what you do.

"Damn, you're really doing this for a living?" I asked him.

"I enjoy it," he said.

It was inspiring to see what he did. It stuck with me. Doing something for someone else and then watching that person strive to get better and do great things. What could be more rewarding than that?

I asked Julian what I needed to do to be able to get this kind of work. He told me to go to school and complete a sociology degree, then work from there. I could go on to get a master's if I wanted, he said.

That was the beginning of my goal to give others the opportunity to succeed, because I'd seen so many without the chances that other kids had.

That's where I got the inspiration to start the Andre De Grasse Family Foundation years later.

But first, it was the reason I chose to study sociology, a field related to social work, as a major when I earned my scholarship to USC. It was really where it all came together. If track didn't work out the way I hoped it would, I was prepared to follow my brother's footsteps into a career that would be as fulfilling and purposeful as I could hope for. That mattered to me.

In the end, it would become a journey that would underpin how I view my place in this world and my responsibility within it.

When I was at USC, I called up my brother to give him a hard time.

"The stuff you do is cool," I said. "But why do I have to write so many damn papers?"

I had to write something like a dozen papers!

"I need you to edit this for me, man," I told him.

He just laughed. I guess that's how my writing finally improved, because I definitely wasn't interested in it before. But there I was, writing long papers.

I didn't enjoy school at all when I was young. I liked the social aspect of it, for sure. I enjoyed being with friends and all the other fun stuff—sports, girls, etc. But actual school is the last thing on your mind when everything else is way more interesting. So I didn't really pay attention in high school at all. I just didn't want to be there. I just didn't want to learn. As I got older, though, I wished I'd understood the value of what I was skipping out on. There are so many things I wish I knew. Things that were actually pretty cool to learn. At the time I wasn't mature enough to see that.

But when I got to college, things changed. It wasn't just that I started to try; it was that I recognized how lucky I was to be there. I genuinely started to enjoy it. I actually enjoyed doing presentations or asking questions in class about topics we were learning about. It was a whole new experience for me, unlocking something inside of myself that I had never tapped into before. I don't know if it was because my brain developed more with age, or if I really did become more mature as a person. But my attitude, my attention, my ability—everything seemed different.

////////

One of the accomplishments in my life that my mother is most proud of is seeing me attend Coffeyville and then move on to USC.

Right after the Rio Olympics, I decided to honour the vow I made to her before I signed with Puma. I knew that if I didn't go back to USC then to complete my degree, I was unlikely to go back at all. It was just going to get harder to complete as I went deeper into my career and adult life.

I was determined to finish what I had started. I wanted to get my degree because it was important for me to know I was more than the athlete everyone now knew me as. USC was still honouring my scholarship, so it was free education at a prestigious private university that cost other people around $75,000 a year to attend. I couldn't let the opportunity to receive a degree from a school like that just slip away. Even if I wanted to, there was no way my mother would have let me.

When I was young, I never saw myself going to university. I thought maybe I'd go to college, but I couldn't see myself being accepted into university. In Ontario high schools at the time, students had to choose between two streams, academic or applied.

While the academic side was intended to prepare students for university, the applied stream focused much more on skills ideal for working in the trades. There was certainly value in that stream of education, but it meant I'd never thought of myself as an "academic."

After a few days of celebrating my Olympic medals with my family and friends, I hopped on a plane to Los Angeles and returned to USC to complete my final semester.

As much as I tried to focus on school that semester, it was hard to take a break from the attention that followed Rio. I hadn't anticipated the demands that came with the exposure of standing on an Olympic podium—or the obligations that came with endorsement deals as a pro athlete. Almost every weekend I was on a plane heading somewhere new.

But on campus, life felt somewhat normal. It's difficult to be a "big deal" at USC—it's a school in Los Angeles; mega celebrities are everywhere and most of my fellow students came from considerable means. Some people stopped to congratulate me on my success at Rio, and a couple of my professors told me they were happy to have me in their class, but otherwise I was just another student trying to keep up. I was happy to be with my friends and classmates, just feeling like a regular young adult again. I needed to work hard to complete my courses that fall. I spent early mornings and long nights at the McKay Center in the Student-Athlete Academic Services office, working with a learning specialist named Marissa, who took the time to make sure I got it right (just like Mrs. Wood had in Coffeyville). It was exhausting and difficult. But we got it done.

I was passionate about what I was learning at USC. It was about more than just receiving a piece of paper. I was still inspired by the work my brother Julian did, and I knew that, in some capacity, I wanted to do something similar.

That semester, I completed my degree in sociology. A younger version of myself, still trying to find his way while finding inspiration in an older brother, would have been proud of who he'd become, on the track and off it. For my mother, completing that degree was as much a cause for celebration as any Olympic medal I could win.

What I had achieved as an athlete would give me a platform. What I learned in the classroom gave me a vision for the good I could do with that platform. Completing my degree that semester was a step towards completing my ongoing growth as a man. I made a commitment to something, and I saw it through.

There is value in finishing what you start. Not just for the achievement, but as an opportunity for lasting growth.

Being asked to deliver the graduation speech at the USC convocation for all the student-athletes at the end of the year was one of the biggest honours of my life. I didn't tell any of my classmates I'd been asked, so I think it was a bit of a surprise for them when I was introduced. I'm an introvert and had never shared much about myself, beyond what people knew about my life as an athlete. But I didn't feel quite as nervous about writing that speech than I might have just a couple years earlier. I'd learned how to express myself. I'd learned to be more confident in my voice and what I had to share with the world. Part of that was the success I had in track and the attention it brought me. But I know a lot of it had to do with my experiences in the classroom, first at Coffeyville and then at USC. I'd expanded my view of the world and gained valuable perspectives I hadn't considered before. And I learned how to express myself in new ways. My education has given me so much more than a piece of paper to validate my accomplishments, in much the same way my medals in track will never define everything I gained from all the work I put into striving for greatness as an athlete. The value is in the pursuit. That's where you grow.

Whenever I speak to young people today, I always stress the importance of working hard in school and getting the best education possible. There are so many benefits to the effort we put into bettering ourselves intellectually and exploring new ideas. The gift of curiosity, the capacity to think critically, and the ability to communicate are all critical to how I carry myself today. Regardless of what you set out to achieve, putting a lifelong education at the forefront of that pursuit will never let you down.

As I was writing out my speech that spring, I noticed my medals from Rio were already scuffed. I realized they were just symbols of a lifelong pursuit. As exciting as it was to have won them, they would never be as lasting and important as the education I'd received at USC and would continue to gain throughout my life.

"Just three years ago I couldn't have imagined competing at the Olympics, let alone winning three medals," I said, as I stood onstage before all my fellow students that day. "And never would I have thought of standing here at this podium at such a distinguished university."

My mother was in the audience, as proud as she'd ever been of me. She'd take so many pictures that day. I'm pretty sure the background photo on her iPhone is still of me posing with her, holding my diploma and my graduation gown.

"There aren't enough things I can say about you," I told my

mom from the podium. "But thank you for always believing in me and being a constant source of motivation and guidance, which have helped me to do my best on and off the track."

What an incredible journey it had been for both of us. There was no way I'd be able to thank her enough.

In that speech, I shared a message that remains one of the most meaningful lessons in my journey so far.

"Records will be broken. Medals will tarnish," I said. "But a university degree is something that nobody can ever take away from me."

It's a lesson I hope anyone who takes the time to read this book and learn about my journey will take with them.

30

PAY IT FORWARD

When I was 18, I earned a spot on the Canadian Pan American Junior Athletics Championships team, which was competing in Colombia.

I was so excited. I made the national team! I'd be representing the entire country. Everyone was happy for me.

But to take the trip my mother and I had to come up with $2,500 to cover the plane tickets and other expenses. That's what the opportunity to represent our country was going to cost.

My mother didn't have that kind of money just sitting around. She had worked so hard just to give me the life we had together. And now, right when this unbelievable opportunity came along, we just couldn't make it work.

But Tony wasn't going to let that happen. Somehow, he found someone to cover the entire fee for me.

I was thrilled. It was the kindest thing anyone had ever done for us.

Because of that gift, I was able to travel to my first international meet, where I ended up winning a bronze in the 100 and a silver in the 200, and that gave me a confidence I'd never had before. I'd represented Canada for the first time and won two medals. I was on top of the world. Suddenly, I started to actually believe what Tony had been telling me. I believed I could make the senior team and that, one day, I might even be able to race in the Olympics.

I've never forgotten that act of kindness and generosity from a stranger. Just like I've never forgotten the many kind things that Tony has done for me through the years, from first giving me a shot in this sport, to believing I could become something special, to following through—being there as a friend and mentor through each and every part of my career.

When I look back at how I was able to achieve my dreams, it's clear to me now that it was only possible because of the sacrifices and generosity of other people. Whether it was my mother, or Tony, or other family and friends along the way.

Without the kindness of others, I probably wouldn't be where I am today. I don't know whether I would have become an Olympic champion. There are so many factors that could have easily tossed this dream off its axis and turned my life into something else entirely.

When I started my foundation in 2018, I did so with that kindness in mind. The mission of the Andre De Grasse Family Foundation is to inspire and empower youth through access to sport, education, and health care. I want to be a role model for kids—and to give them resources so they can chase their own dreams. Hopefully, they can pay that forward to someone else.

One of the best lessons I've learned about achieving success is that the most fulfilling part is finding a way to help someone else do the same. It's a lesson that Julian showed me when he told me how good helping someone else can make you feel. You can put your mind to something and reach those goals, but putting your heart into it is what makes it feel so wonderful. I think any pursuit that doesn't have kindness as an underlying principle is wasted, because I know first-hand what that kind of kindness can mean for a person.

※※※

I often think about the bigger picture.

What is the purpose of all of this, really? What is the actual value of the years spent on the track, in a constant race that I know I'll never be fully satisfied with. That's the nature of the sport—glory and disappointment. There is a thrill that comes with that. There is real passion, pain, and joy. But when it's all over, what will it have meant? Will it have done any good?

I want other people to be able to pursue their dreams the way I've been able to. For me, that's the bigger picture. It's knowing that without the generosity of other people, I wouldn't have become an Olympic champion—and I wouldn't be writing this book. So many of the things that have lined up in my life likely wouldn't have happened. I simply wouldn't be doing what I'm doing today if someone else hadn't done what they did back then.

Without that spark, so many dreams fail to take flight.

I know there are many other kids like that out there—kids like me—who might have the talent but don't have that opportunity.

But if I can provide support for them to get to that next

level, then maybe we'll start to hear of more Andre De Grasses out there—more of the otherwise unknown, making a name for themselves.

I need to return the favour—pay it forward—because it's the most valuable thing I can do with the success I've had.

Recently, I was honoured as Athlete of the Year at the first-ever Legacy Awards, an event created to celebrate Black excellence and achievement. We never had an awards show like that before in Canada, celebrating Black achievement specifically. It was awesome. It was a real honour. And stepping back, I believe it was great for the Black community as well as society as a whole. It's good for our kids—it'd be good for *my* kids, for *any* kids—to look up and say, "I can do this. I can do whatever I dream of becoming and work hard to achieve, regardless of what anyone else might think of me." It doesn't have to be sports. It can be anything.

We have a long way to go.

The Legacy Awards were inspiring. I was so proud and so humbled to be in that room with so many incredible people.

It reminded me of why the foundation is so meaningful to me. When I started my foundation, I wanted to focus on helping anybody who needed support.

In 2017, with the help of my closest friends, we started the Andre De Grasse Holiday Classic basketball tournament. It supports my charity but also gives me an opportunity to go back home and meet hundreds of kids and maybe inspire them a little bit. I'm glad we're able to return to the sport in which it all started to help pass it on to the next generation, in the spirit in which we all fell in love with sports to begin with.

In track, my old coach Tony Sharpe always tells me there are so many talented kids out there. They just need the opportunity, but they don't always get it. We started the Future Champions Fund to try to target those kids specifically and to inspire and empower the next generation in the sport with the resources and guidance they need to reach their own unique potential on and off the track. We want to make sure that no one is left behind.

Knowing we've been able to make so many young people become better athletes, by covering all the costs and providing expert training and guidance so they can reach the next level on the track, is something that means a lot to me. After just a few years, we've had some athletes go on to university or college. It's an amazing feeling. Julian was right. You can actually see that it really worked. When I find out that another kid has earned a university or college scholarship, it feels as thrilling as a win.

And then you see the smiles on their faces, the absolute joy. And it seems so familiar. It's like a reflection in a mirror from the not-too-distant past.

///////

I always read books to my daughter Yuri before bedtime. It's one of my favourite things to share with her. One night, during the pandemic in 2020, as we flipped through another tale, I decided I wanted to write a children's book too. I thought it would be fun for Yuri to be able to read about her dad the way we explored other stories together. And I wanted to give kids some hope and some inspiration, especially during the challenges of the pandemic, when so many were isolated from school and sports. I've always felt so lucky for the opportunities I've had through track. Sports had been so fundamental to my development as a young person, and I wanted kids to know they could find meaning and hope through sports the same way I had.

I contacted a publisher, found a writer to work with, and soon I was working on my very first book. We called it *Race with Me!* It is an inspirational kids book about my journey and what it's like to be on the starting line on race day.

"When I run, I feel free," I wrote on the first page.

I want children to understand the joy that comes with running and other sports. I want them to be able to experience the thrill of competition and the feeling of accomplishment that comes with realizing just how much they are capable of. The story explores my unlikely journey to becoming an Olympic medallist. The book ends with a message that I hope inspires kids to believe nothing is impossible: "See it, believe it!"

It means a lot to me to know that kids can learn about my story and that I might have a positive influence on them. Especially now, when life has been incredibly hard for so many young people.

Having my own children made me reflect on what it's like to be a kid. Even though they were still too young to really be affected by the pandemic, it wasn't hard to see how difficult life would have been for them if they were just a little bit older.

The book was a great way to share that message, but I wanted to take it a step further. In the months before the book was set to come out, in the midst of the global pandemic, I was contacted by a young teenager in Montreal named Jesse Briscoe who was frustrated by the cancellation of his sports clubs during the pandemic and was getting tired of sitting around all day watching TV and playing video games. We wanted to help get other kids like him off the couch—feeling the freedom and joy that comes with being active. Jesse and his family came up with the concept of a virtual challenge to get people across Canada active after enduring more than a year of restrictions and the devastating effects of the pandemic on the physical and mental health of so many people. Jesse reached out to me because he'd been inspired by what I had done in track and by my desire to motivate young people.

We called it the Race with Me! virtual challenge. For eight consecutive weeks, participants were encouraged to go to their local 400-metre track and run one lap as fast as they could and return week after week. It was just a simple way to get kids out of the house and away from their screens. It took off!

When we were looking for charities to partner with, Kids Help Phone immediately came to mind. The pandemic had taken such a toll on kids and their mental health. We wanted to do what we could to support a cause that could help some young people through those challenges.

Thousands of people across the country took part in the challenge, from kids all the way up to people as old as 82. When I returned from the Olympics, we organized an event at one of the schools I attended in Markham, joined by Jesse, the CEO of Kids Help Phone, and some of the kids who raced in the virtual challenge. It was a small "big" event in an open space at the school, with everyone involved wearing masks. It still felt like a surreal world, but I think the challenge helped life feel a little bit more normal for everyone who took part, at least for a time. Until the moment I got to meet the kids who participated it hadn't felt entirely real.

We ended up raising $25,000 for Kids Help Phone through the program and helped inspire people to stay active and take care of their physical and mental health. It was a thrill to see everything come together so well. It meant so much to me to be able to use my platform for something positive. When my career is over, I hope I'll have done as much as I can to pay this unlikely dream forward to as many people as possible. It's about more than a responsibility. It's about the joy of gratitude—and the feeling that you've made a positive difference in the world.

I think of someone like Jesse, who came up with a wonderful idea and had the courage to reach out and pursue it. That's inspiring. You don't need to have a large platform to make a difference. You don't need to have a million Instagram followers or to have made a lot of money. Everyone who took part in the Race with Me! challenge played a role in the program's success.

Sometimes we can be so consumed by the pursuit of greatness that we lose sight of what greatness actually is. It's about so much more than what you achieve. True greatness is about how you use your skills and privileges to help others get ahead. There are few things in life that will bring you more joy than knowing that, in some way, you've done that for someone else.

////////

After winning gold in Tokyo, I've thought a lot about what it all means. I've thought a lot about my legacy, and how, when it's all done, I hope people will remember me.

The medals are great. Winning is great. I always love the thrill of the chase. But after Tokyo—and after all the challenges of the few years that came before—I've realized that my life needs to carry more than just victories on the track.

What do I want to be known for? Do I want to be known for

winning medals? Do I want people to say I was once the fastest guy in the world? Yes—of course I want that. But, just as much, I want to be known as a guy who was genuine. A guy who helped out a lot of people, who was inspirational to others in so many different ways, because others cared enough to do that for him.

If we're going to chase extraordinary goals in our lives, I think we need to start with an extraordinary sense of purpose. Not only for what is possible to achieve on our own, but for what that pursuit will mean for the next generation, chasing us from behind.

31

FIND VICTORY IN EVERYTHING

I can't run forever. I don't want to be the person who tries. I'm on the verge of competing in my third Olympics in the summer of 2024. I feel like I'm still young. And I am, by most standards. But in track I'm reaching my prime. That's exciting, but I know what's on the other side.

I feel like I still have a lot left in me to accomplish. But I'll be almost 30 years old in 2024 when I try to defend my gold medal in Paris. I know that doesn't seem very old in the real world, but in sprinting, it's the beginning of the end.

I don't know what lies ahead for me beyond Paris. It depends on so many things that are out of my control. If my body holds up, I hope to reach at least one more Olympic Games.

Los Angeles would be a fitting place for this dream to end. It's where it first really took off when I landed that scholarship at USC and where my first coach, Tony Sharpe, ran at his first Olympics. Those college days seem so far away now.

So maybe I'll make it to 2028. Maybe even beyond.

I'll never put a cap on what's possible. But I've learned to put a cap on what I need. At this point of my career, I've learned to be satisfied with what I've achieved. That doesn't mean I don't want to keep winning—or that I'm any less competitive than I've ever been. But if Tokyo gave me anything, it was one less thing to prove.

I'll keep going as long as I am capable and still have the necessary drive. But I know the end will come sooner than later. And when it's finally time for me to hang up my spikes, I'll be ready.

In any pursuit of excellence, it's important to always remember that there will be an end. No one stays on top forever, but we can at least try to go out on top.

That's why we strive to be the best we can, always pushed by those whose time to win will inevitably come.

A decade ago, I set out to be one of the fastest people in the world and to win an Olympic gold medal. I realized that dream at the Tokyo Olympics. A whole lot of life happened along the way. I've thought a lot about what matters to me beyond the track. I've thought a lot about what I want to do when the opportunities on the track are gone.

One of the hardest lessons I've learned in my career is not how to achieve greatness but instead how to let it go. When my time to run is done, I'll be ready to walk away.

Yes, your career matters. You want to be successful and to provide the best life possible for yourself and your loved ones. But in the end, the most valuable thing you can attain is the love and support of the people around you.

That's what matters. Surround yourself with the people who

really mean something to you. All the people that make life fun, that make it better. The people who make life worth living. You can win all the medals and make all the money in the world. But if you don't have people around you to love and share it with, it's not the same.

You want to share that moment and share that glory with them. If you focus on just career, career, career—or success, success, success—you might be miserable.

We've got to keep life in perspective.

I try my best to live in the moment, because in the back of my mind I know nothing is a given.

So as much as I will work hard and continue to be the best I can, I'm not thinking about my future the same way I used to. I'm a dad now—and track is my job. I run for my kids. I run to provide for my family. I run for pride and the drive of competition too, but I'm no longer looking forward to what I need to accomplish with blinders on.

I'm preparing for Paris, but I'm not obsessing about it. My career has taught me a lot. I'm trying to find joy in the hard work, lessons in the losses, and gains from what might seem like a setback.

Each race is a building block for the next goal. Each race is a moment to enjoy because there will come a day when I won't be able to do this anymore.

One day, I'll be something else. I'll have to be. And I'm dreaming of those possibilities now. Because even now, I'm much more than Andre De Grasse *the sprinter*. There is so much that I can do, so many other things I want to be.

I've seen people become so consumed by the one thing they do that they can't see themselves as anything beyond that. They get so invested in their craft that they can't imagine a world without it.

I'm invested in my craft; I have a great passion for track. But I won't be held captive by it. So I take time to imagine the future—to dream of other things.

What do I want to do? What do I want to give my time to? What else do I want to learn?

A career in sports teaches you so much if you're willing to apply those lessons beyond the track, field, or arena. When you go out into the real world, you're confident. You have leadership skills. And the ability to communicate. But athletes can often struggle when they make the transition to regular life. It can be difficult to find a sense of purpose after dedicating so much of your life to something you can longer do.

I think it's imperative for all of us, whatever we do, to focus on being well-balanced people who are able to find joy and meaning in many pursuits.

I've been thinking a lot lately about what I might become. Maybe I'll be an agent one day. I've always enjoyed the business side of sport. I can see myself working with athletes the way Paul and Brian work with me. I've learned so much about that world through all the work my team does for me—and I find it fascinating.

Or maybe I'll do something less conventional and finish that dream of playing pro hoops. I'll try out to join the Canadian Basketball League, like J. Cole recently did. Who knows?

Maybe I'll focus on my foundation full time and work closely with organizations that can use the kind of love and support I've been blessed with in my life. Perhaps I'll do more speaking events, which I've come to enjoy.

There are so many possibilities. I can see them all. Whatever I decide to do, I'll pursue it with the same passion that I run with today.

I'll try to find victory in everything I do.

Right now, though, I just want to live well and enjoy my family. I want to watch my kids grow. I want to watch them laugh, love, and learn. I want to see them discover their own dreams and strive for greatness in the pursuit of them.

There will be a time for Paris, and maybe a time for LA. But there will be dozens of unmissable moments in between. So I'm going to focus on the little, important things first.

I hope you will too.

THE RUNDOWN

In the pursuit of our goals, we all make choices that will either help or hurt our ability to hit the targets we set for ourselves. Below are some of the principles that have helped me find success on the track and in life.

Find a rhythm of life that works for you. Keep disappointment and success in perspective, knowing that more of each will come regardless of what you do.

Don't let self-restricting emotions block you. You will never know your full potential if you don't make the choice to believe you can achieve great things.

Write out your goals. Make them known as an exercise of action and purpose in your life. Work with intention, and be diligent about the plan you set out. Say it loud. Make it real. And then set out to achieve it.

Use disappointment to propel you forward. Leave defeat in the past. Don't dwell on it, unless you're revisiting what you can learn from the experience.

Set out to achieve your goals each day. End each day knowing you've racked up another win in whichever areas of life where you hope to achieve success. If you stay focused on those efforts, success will follow.

Turn pressure and criticism into positive motivation. Find a balance between the outside expectations and the criticism that follow success.

Appreciate the people who gave you a path to pursue your dreams. It's very rare for someone to achieve excellence on their own.

Doubting your capability before you even try is accepting defeat. The only opinion that matters when it comes to achieving peak performance is yours.

To have success, you need to drown out the distractions, both internal and external. And remember that regardless of what it is you are competing in, *you* are your toughest competitor.

Failing to prepare is preparing to fail. Regardless of your specific goals, you need to put in the time and effort to ensure that you are at your best when it comes time to perform.

Make focus a priority that you refuse to waver from. Focus is a key element in achieving peak performance. Our routines put us in the mental space we need to be in to be our best.

After achieving success, step back and assess how to best chase your next goals. That process requires rest and rebuilding. It's key to being ready for what comes next.

Know your own worth. Don't be tempted by the first offer that comes along or feel pressured into acting without considering the other potential outcomes. Do the work to find out what you're worth, and have the confidence to ask for it.

Be mindful with money. Regardless of how much money you make, be careful with how you use what you earn, and be diligent about managing with the future in mind.

Remember that the impression we make defines who we are to others. To make a lasting impression, show people that you value their time and that you take your commitments seriously.

Understand yourself and how you learn. Reflect on what has worked before and what hasn't. We all learn, find motivation, and are inspired in different ways.

Avoid being distracted by the noise of competition. Personal conflict has nothing to do with achieving your goal. It's about you being your best. That's the only thing that matters.

Unite with your team. The best teams support each other and push each other forward, getting the best out of every person. They become one body, racing towards the same goal.

When everything else is gone, we're left with what actually matters. What is that for you? And who is it? Find hope and strength in those answers.

Be critical of your comfort zone. Comfort can be a barrier to success if you're not careful. To find success, you need to be aware of what is working and what isn't—be willing to make the necessary changes to get where you want to be.

Believe and persist. Believing you deserve to achieve a goal, whether by destiny or will, is so important. But without a deliberate, constant effort to achieve it, that goal will never be reached.

Go slow, now and then. So many of us spend our days speeding past the good parts of life, moving from one obligation to the next. In a fast life, it's easy to lose focus on why we're running in the first place. Sometimes it's helpful to just slow down.

Get the balance right. When you achieve something you've worked hard for, part of you should be able to celebrate that and find joy in it. But another part of you, the relentlessly competitive perfectionist part of you, knows you could do better. Find the balance between both.

Find a support system of people who have a positive influence on you. Lean on them when things aren't going right. We don't achieve anything alone.

Focus on your nutrition, hydration, and sleep. Make those healthy choices a daily habit. Let those healthy habits give you the strength and energy to be your best.

Never define yourself by what you have achieved or by what you are yet to achieve. Instead, be proud of what you've done to stand where you do—and remember how far you've come to get there.

Life is never too busy for you to make space for the people you love. Nothing you accomplish can compare to the happiness that being with those people will give you.

Pace yourself. Keep a healthy balance of time and energy management by setting your priorities and compartmentalizing your schedules.

Prioritize education. The gift of curiosity, the capacity to think critically, and the ability to communicate are all critical to success. Regardless of what you set out to achieve, putting a lifelong education at the forefront of that pursuit will never let you down.

True greatness is using your skills and privileges to help others. There are few things in life that will bring you more joy than knowing that, in some way, you've done that for someone else.

Make room for your whole self. We can become so consumed by the one thing we do that we can't see ourselves as anything beyond that. Real victory is found in being a well-balanced person who is able to find joy and meaning in many pursuits.

ACKNOWLEDGEMENTS

I'm grateful to the family and friends who have loved and supported me throughout my life. Thank you for believing in me. Thank you for helping me through the highs and lows of this journey. Thank you for your hard work, sacrifice, and dedication in helping me persevere. You've each played a part in making my dreams possible. —ADG

Thank you to HarperCollins Canada for bringing this book to life. To Jim Gifford for your vision and guidance throughout this process. To Noelle Zitzer, Brad Wilson, and the entire HarperCollins team for all your work behind the scenes to make this possible. We're especially indebted to Patricia MacDonald for her careful edits and thoughtful suggestions. And thank you to Rick Broadhead for your enthusiasm for this project and continued guidance as a literary agent. To Brian Levine and the team at Envision Sports & Entertainment: thank you for your input and support from start to finish. And thank you, Andre, for sharing your experiences and insights with these readers—and for trusting me to help you do that. —DR

NOTES

Page 46—**"I'm just so happy . . ."**: After winning the bronze medal in the 100 metres at the World Championships in Beijing, I was interviewed by Sweden's SVT, during which Usain Bolt stopped in to congratulate me. The interview was broadcast by the CBC on August 23, 2015.

Page 49—**"I never thought . . ."**: I was interviewed by Grant Robertson of the *Globe and Mail* ahead of the Rio Olympics and spoke about competing against Usain Bolt in an article titled "Canadian sprinter Andre De Grasse aiming to go toe-to-toe with Usain Bolt," published in that newspaper on August 12, 2016.

Page 50—**"It's always good to see . . ."**: Usain Bolt was interviewed before the 100-metre event at the Rio Olympics and said that I reminded him of a younger version of himself. His comments were published by the Canadian Press.

Page 50—**"For me, De Grasse has shown . . ."**: Usain Bolt was interviewed in a press conference after the 100-metre final at the Rio Olympics. His comments referring to me and "the future of the sport is in good hands" were reported by Vicki Hall and published in the *National Post* on August 15, 2016.

Page 52—**"This brotherhood continues . . .":** The 200-metre semifinal at the Rio Olympics was broadcast live by the CBC, after which the play-by-play announcer said, "This brotherhood continues," following my close finish with Usain Bolt. The broadcast aired live on August 17, 2016.

Page 52—**"It's just one of those things . . .":** Bolt's comments about my effort to win the 200-metre semifinal at the Rio Olympics were reported by Reuters and published by the *Sydney Morning Herald* on August 18, 2016.

Page 200—**"If you asked me . . .":** My interview with Scott Russell was broadcast by the CBC after the World Championship 100-metre final on September 28, 2019.

Page 225—**They watched from the . . . :** My interview with Adrienne Arsenault after winning gold in the 200 metres at the Tokyo Olympics was broadcast by the CBC on August 4, 2021.

Page 228—**"I know how hard . . .":** My mother, Beverley, was interviewed on the CBC Radio program *As It Happens*, reacting to my gold medal victory on August 4, 2021.